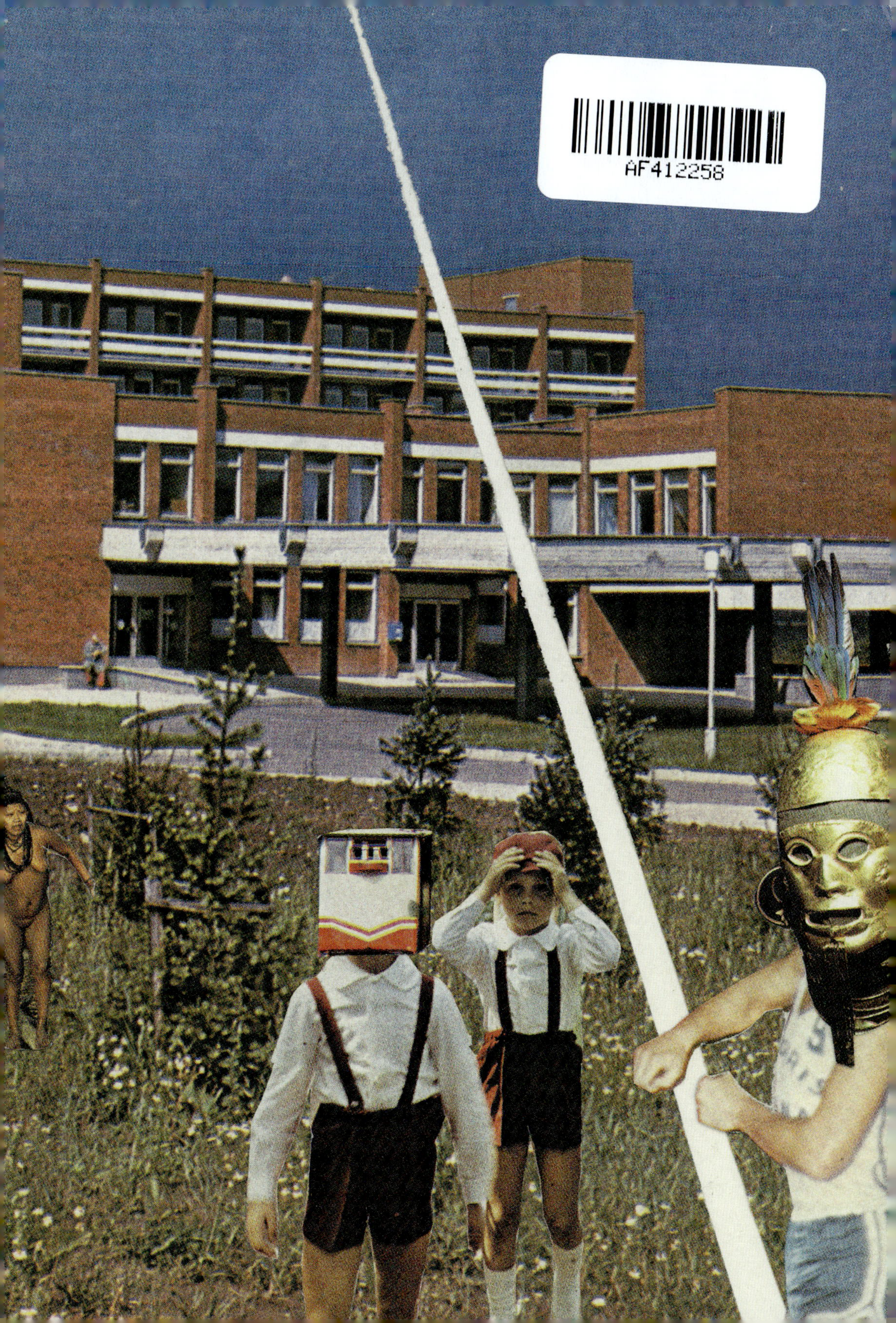
AF412258

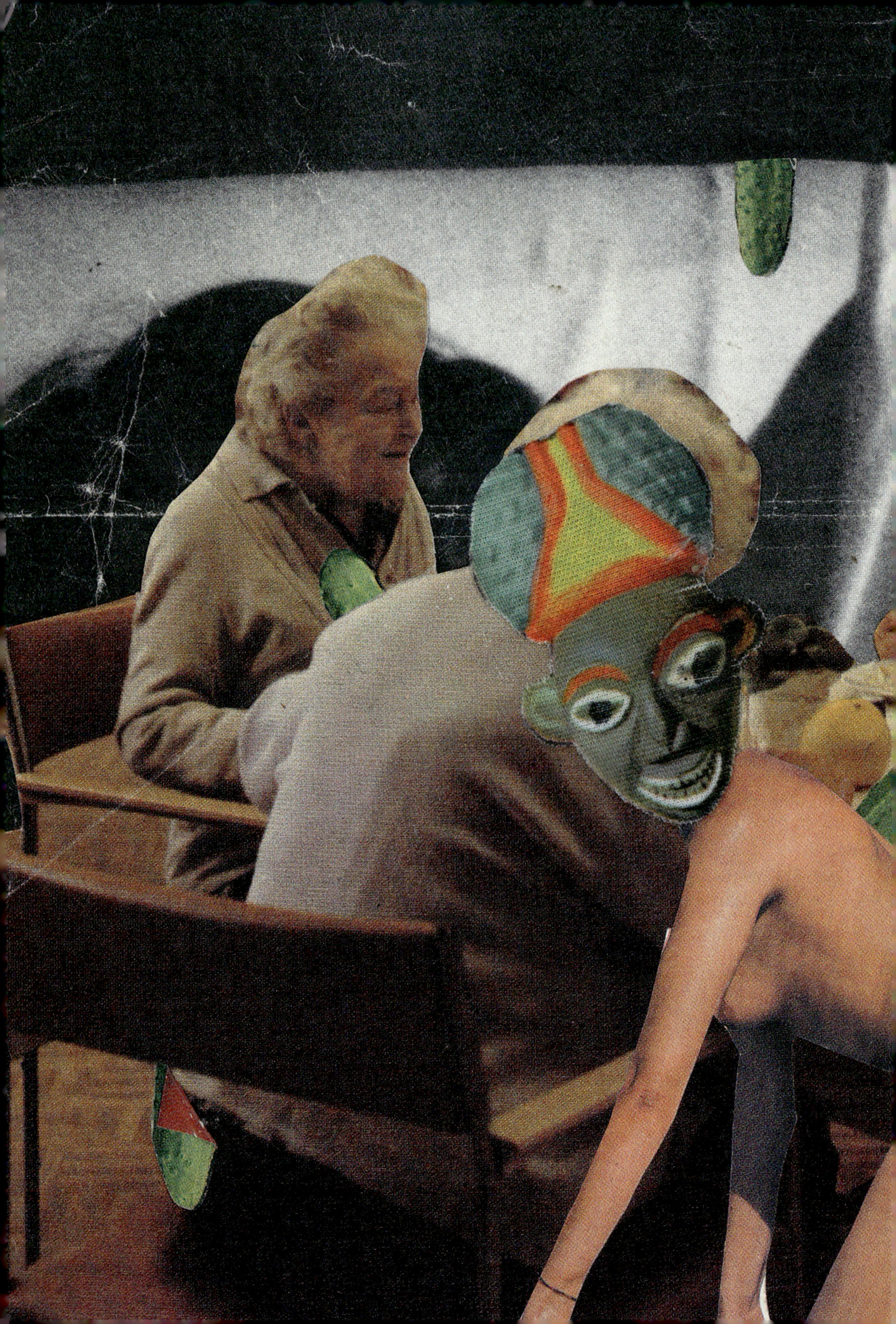

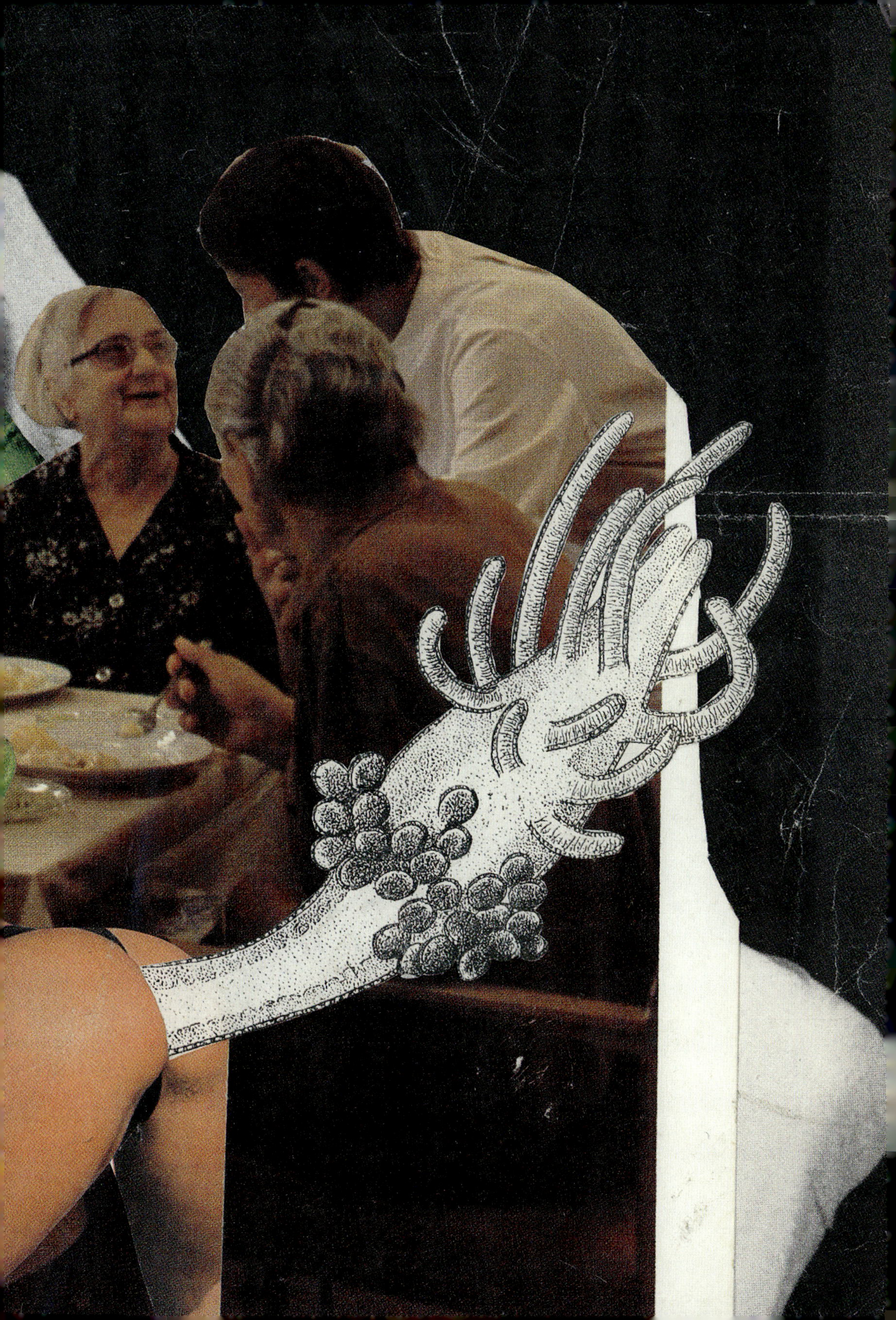

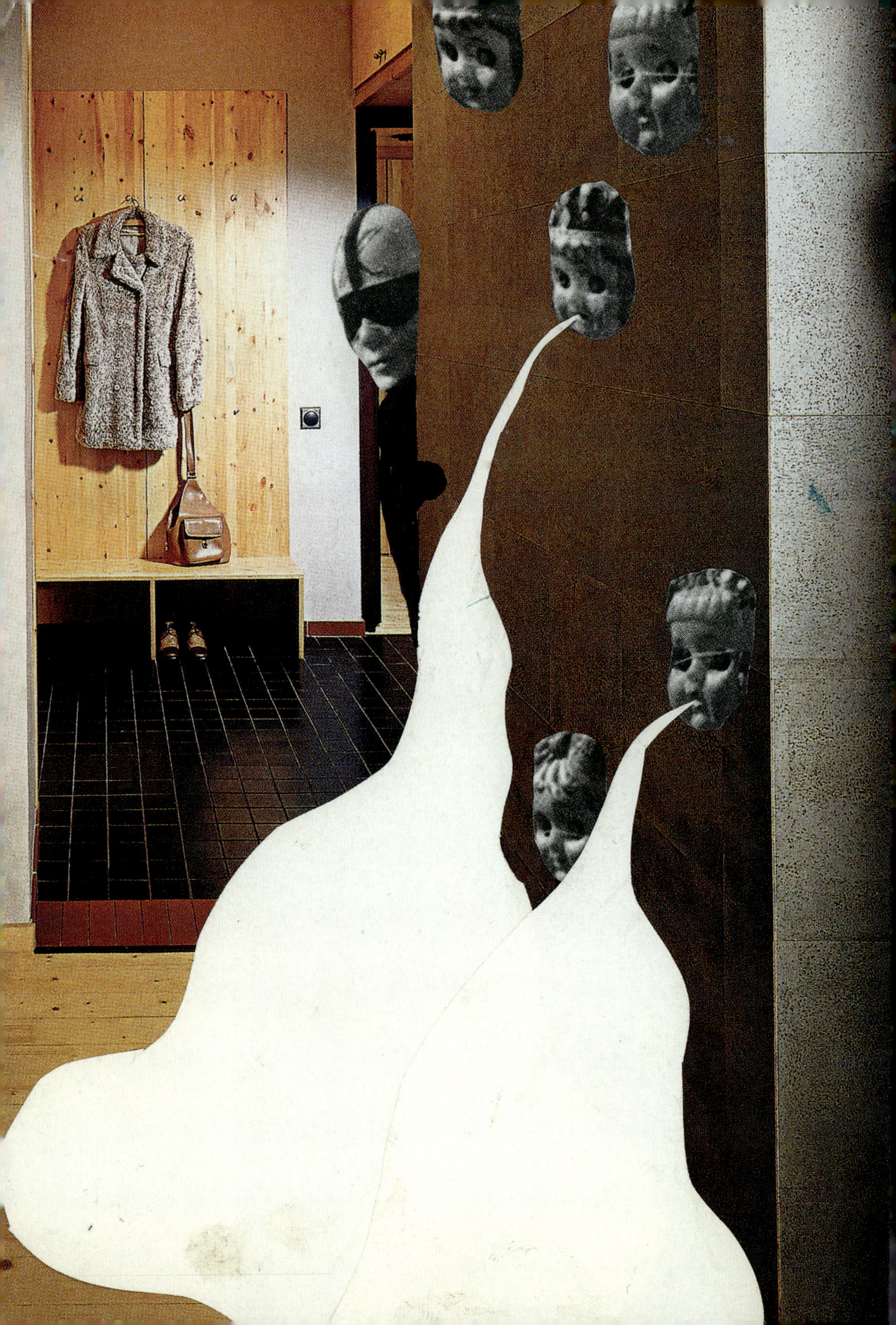

Henri Bergson likes to grimace. He says the comic spirit houses a sound logic, is a robust practice, but careful he says, for the comic spirit has no scruples.

Welcome to 'Tolstoyevsky', issue 10 of *The Happy Hypocrite*, guest-edited by Virginija Januškevičiūtė.

Now, whilst the comic spirit may be without scruples, may be immoral, we could never say that it is truly *wrong*, that is, there is no wrong way to laugh at a joke. Even though Immanuel Kant says 'Laughter is the result of an expectation, which, of a sudden, ends in nothing', the recital of felt laughter, of concomitant joy, cannot be rehearsed, always happens in real-time, generatively.

Each issue of *The Happy Hypocrite* is themed by method, not by subject matter; Virginija's tall tale of Tolstoyevsky – as related in the outro, and on the back cover of this journal – synchronises class aspiration with ragged performativity in a bathetic way. Denise Riley says 'There is sound sense in attending to your own nagging embarrassment. With linguistic embarrassment in general, you intuit that under the chivvying of standard talk, you're about to be forcibly revealed.'

Virginija draws our attention to the raised edges of the realm of the sensible. What's under it is not easy. Most meaning is not neatly made.

—Maria Fusco

5

Introduction
Maria Fusco

8

Moles & Mice
Candice Lin

25

In The Beginning
Kim Schoen

27

Moves Between Light
Zoe Kingsley

37

Morta Della
Michael Lawton

40

The Oldest Woman
Jonas Žakaitis
Translated from Lithuanian by Erika Lastovskyte

44

Restaurant Sankt Peterburgas
Jonas Žakaitis
Translated from Lithuanian by Erika Lastovskyte

49

Cemetery Detective
Monika Kalinauskaitė
Translated from Lithuanian by Erika Lastovskyte

51

Rauschenberg & Brexit Are Braving the Surf
Isabel Waidner

54

Shooting Stars
David Bernstein

64

Only One Silver Teapot
Nick Norton

70

Say What You See/See What You Hear
Answers to pp. 92–94, The Happy Hypocrite
#ACCUMULATOR_PLUS, Issue 9
Tai Shani/Jlin

72

Outro
Virginija Januškevičiūtė

Candice Lin

Moles & Mice

1

I had a friend who grew envious when
I admitted to him that, embarrassingly, my
partner and I had devolved a kind of intimate
home way of talking (about the dishes,
feeding the cat, or paying the bills and other
banal domesticities) in high-pitched 'mouse'
voices ● 'I want to be a mouse too!'
he cried out indignantly ● And from that
moment on he was a mouse too ●

'Hey mouse, do you want to go to Super
Stop-n-Shop later today?'

2

‘ Mouse! Look mouse, I found a rock that
looks like meat ● Here, take it, it’s for
you mouse ● ’

‘ What should my new book be called? ’

‘ Anymouse ’

‘ E A M O Y mouse ● ’
(peals of mouse laughs)

Language had become laden with privacy
that gave the mice a soft, secret laughter
together, and it warmed their respective
burrows ● Across the grey prairie, across the
back of a whale, over a long quiet sea seen
from a distance, I text him a message that
simply reads ‘ Oh mouse! ’ and he replies,
‘ Mouse, mouse! How are you mouse? ’
I remember well the many meat rocks
he gave me but also the lichen he did not ●

3

In Texas, muskrats line their burrows with
found fur and plants sterilised in their urine,
and this calcifies into a thin vegetal shell
which botanists extract in cross-sections
to determine the extinction rate, or at least,
the way certain plants are moving to lower
altitudes with the changing climate ●

I had a dream that a mouse was burrowing
into my intestines and when I woke and wrote
you, you replied, ❛ that's strange, I have been
having health issues down there, but don't
worry, they are mostly past now ● ❜ The
words ❛ health issues ❜ takes me nine months
to digest and when I reply it is only to say,
❛ I'm sorry I have not replied sooner, I have
been so busy ● ❜ And then ● ● ● one year
later, more frantically ● ● ● ❛ How is your
health? You are okay, aren't you? No mouse
got you? ❜ Mouse becomes code for health
trouble, for impending death ●

4

Today I learned that synthetic cinnabar,
vermilion, was made from sulphur and
mercury crushed and heated together. This
was mixed with lizards pounded in a marble
mortar ● They were still alive and squirming
under the pestle as it came down relentlessly
with its overwhelming weight (like the heavy
bodies of lesbians at queer pagan camp,
like how I imagine the hammer came down
on the woman's skull in the podcast I listened
to earlier) but it did not matter, they were
just like so many ❛ slugs-with-eyes ❜ that
my mom killed with kleenex in our rainy
basement ● Some were so large that, at
last, she felt some remorse: ❛ They were
really too big to be killed in that way, with
only a tissue between it and my hand ● ❜

At the Getty, a screaming child dragged
against the hand of her mother, ❛ I hate you,
I hate you, you are killing me ● ❜ And I was

reminded of our earlier tense drive to the
museum where I had said in response to my
mother's suggestion that she live with me
for a month, ❛ That might be disastrous. ❜
And she, hurt and quiet, said, ❛ Oh does
this daughter also feel she cannot stand her
mother? ❜ and I said, ❛ No no I love you but
● ● ● ❜ haltingly, ❛ ● ● ● I do feel judged
all the time and it's ● ● ● hard to live like
that ● You are critical you know, you say
so yourself ● ❜ And she, looking through her
purse desperately for what she had forgotten,
in a little voice, ❛ Oh, am I? am I? ❜

It is the skeleton that creates the sensation
of pain, for did you ever hear of a burlap
bag without broken glass crying or singing
tragic songs? I'm not referring to the hernia
you ignored as a child or the ulcer that gives
you acne, but the structure, the family, the
content that fits sharply but in no possible

other way, inside the rough skin you call
your own ● But this red, reptilian mixture,
this fake cinnabar, known as guard chamber,
was dotted on the Emperor's concubines to
corral their bodies ● In theory, the red dot
could turn dark bluish-black ● These moles
became very fashionable.

Replications of them were made of velvet
and mouse ●

They were called ❛ flies ❜ and perhaps the
French women of court who wore them
were corpses just beginning to rot ● These
fashion moles in different positions on their
face meant specific things: under the nose
to the right meant, ❛ No dear, not tonight ❜
while the one perched loftily on her forehead
signalled to another lover, ❛ I will leave
him in four days, wait for me on the edge
of the woods ● ❜

7

In the 1700s the Spanish Benedictine friar
Benito Jeronimo Feijoo had a theory that
the origin of racial blackness stemmed
from ❛ a tiny black spot on a man's genitals
and on the fingernails of both men and
women ❜ ● This black spot grew larger
and larger until it encompassed the whole
genitalia, all the fingers, and up the palm to
the forearms, shoulders and down the back ●

I am reminded of my childhood where,
during my Chinese indoctrination, I was
given Amy Tan's *Joy Luck Club* to read along
with *Wild Swans* and *The Rape of Nanking* ●
In the story, one mother tells her daughter
how she escaped an arranged marriage by
making up a story that the black mole on
her child-husband's back would grow larger
and larger until it swallowed him and all
his unborn babies up ● I am thinking about
my skin flipping back upon itself with a

8

darkness that engulfs ● The exterior becomes
an interior, a dark cave, and a mole becomes,
not a ‘ fly ’ or a secret message or a
devouring mouth, but simply the animal,
blind and groping in a tunnel of dirt ●

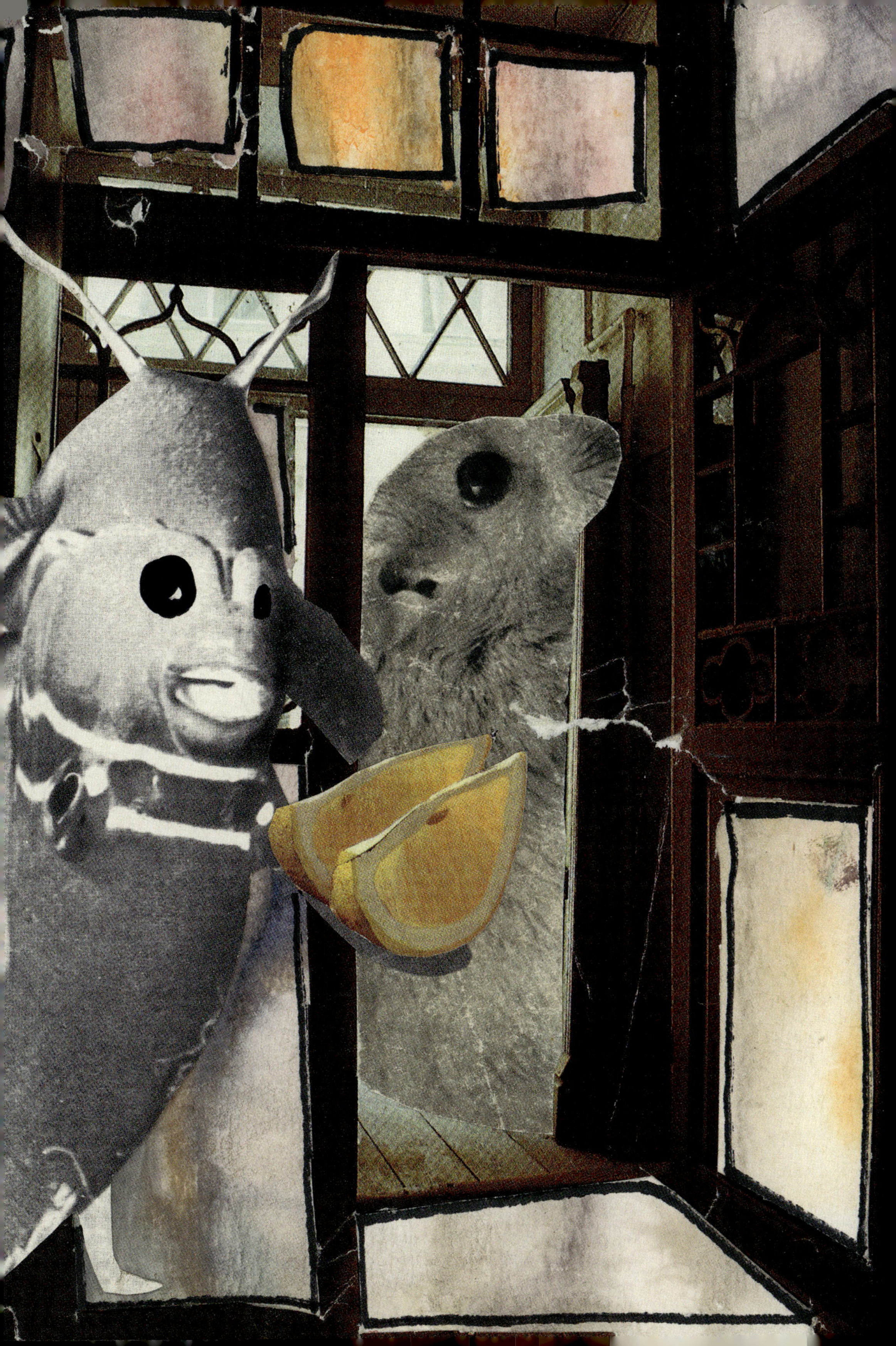

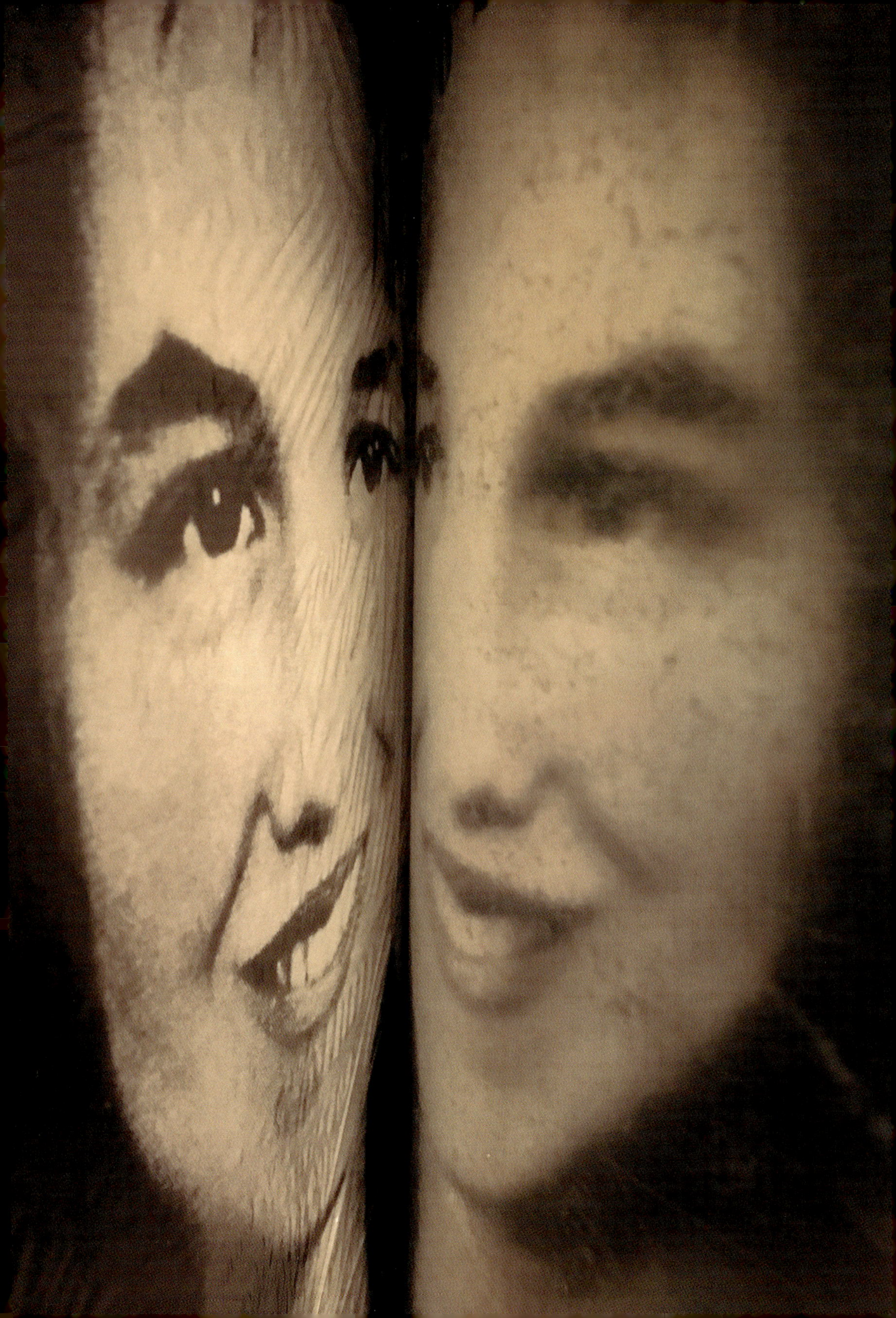

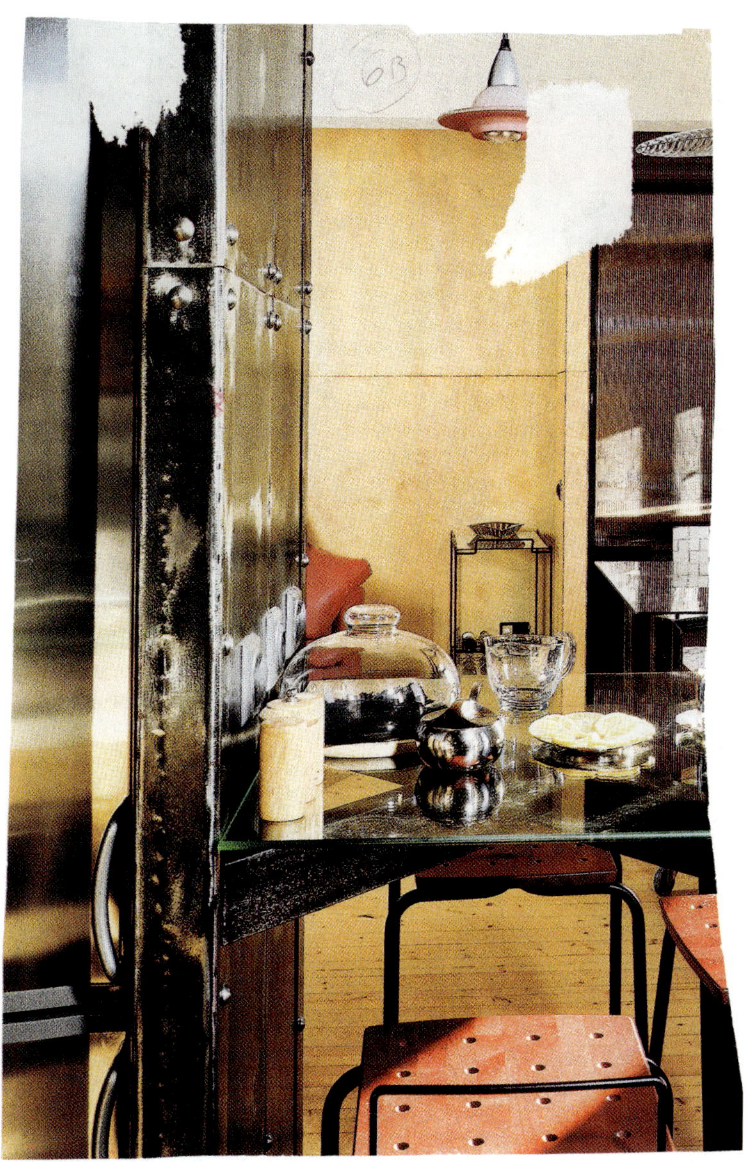

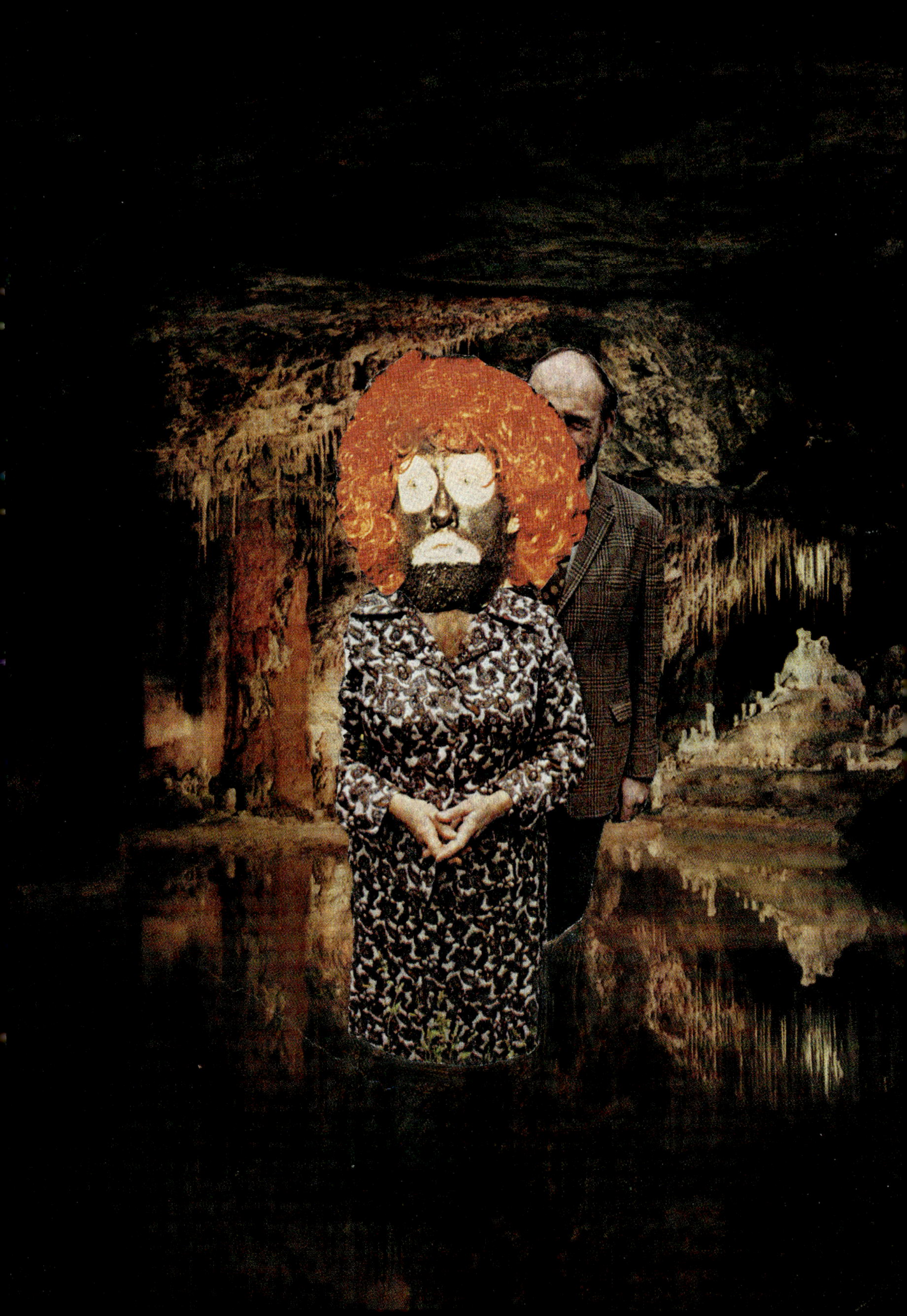

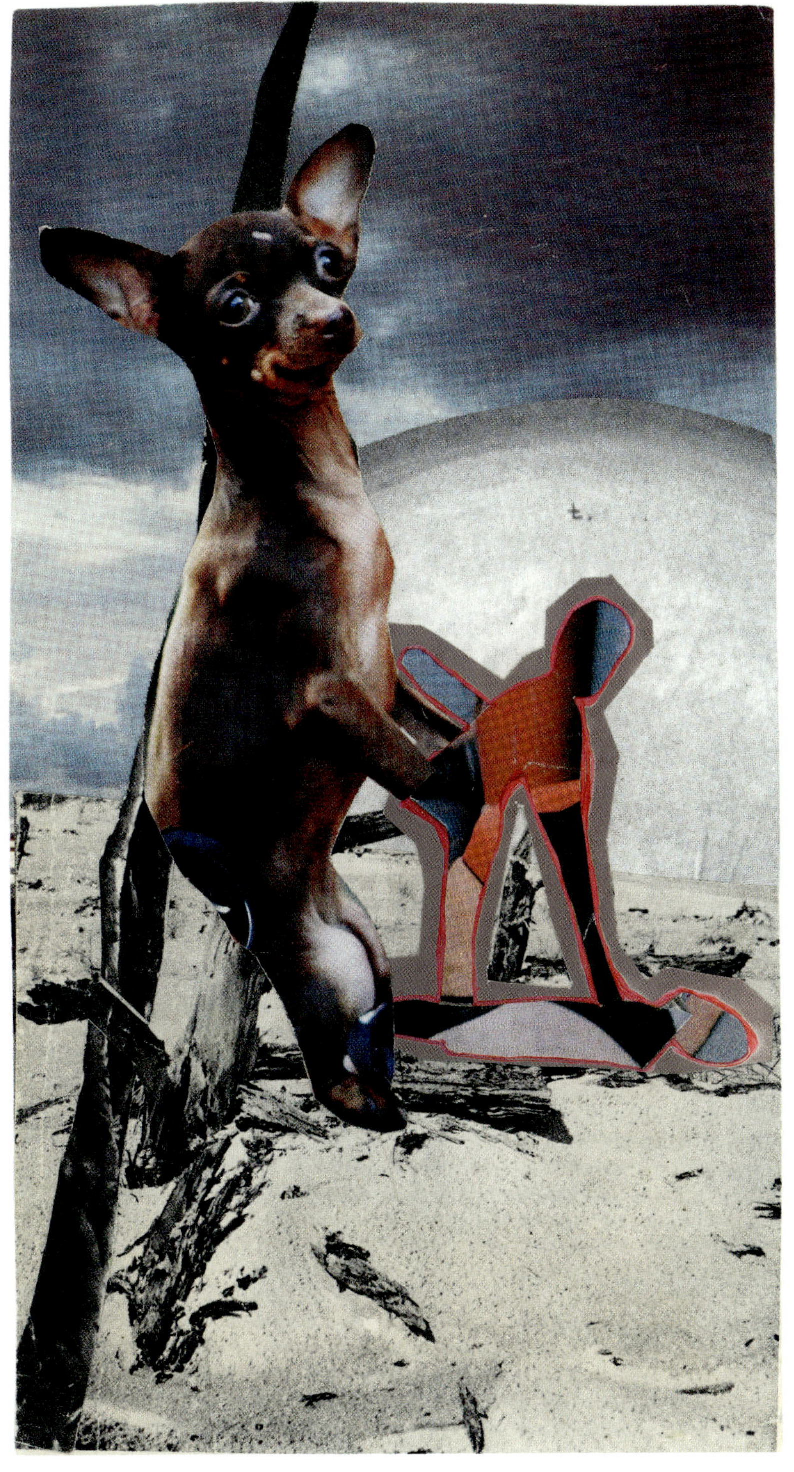

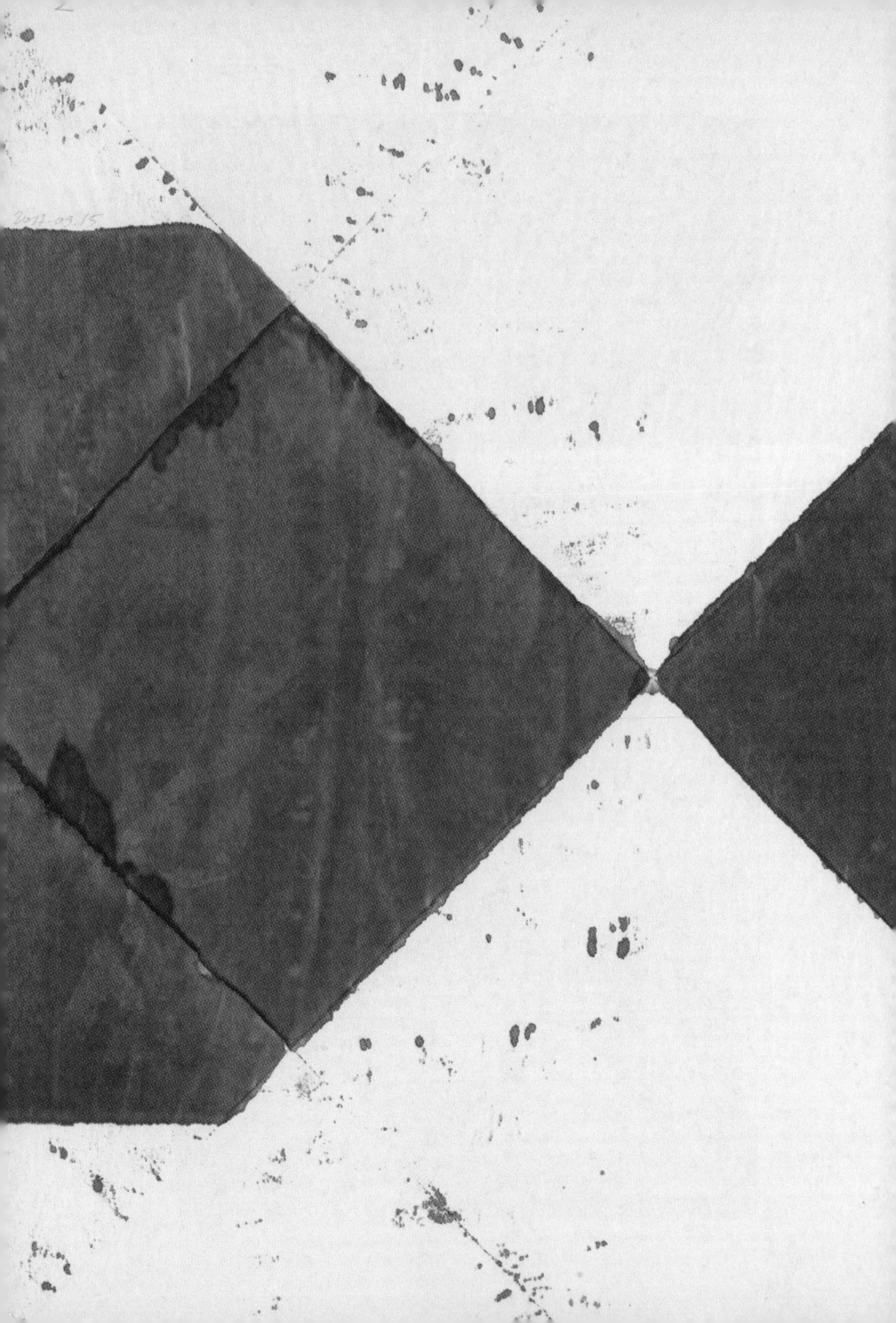

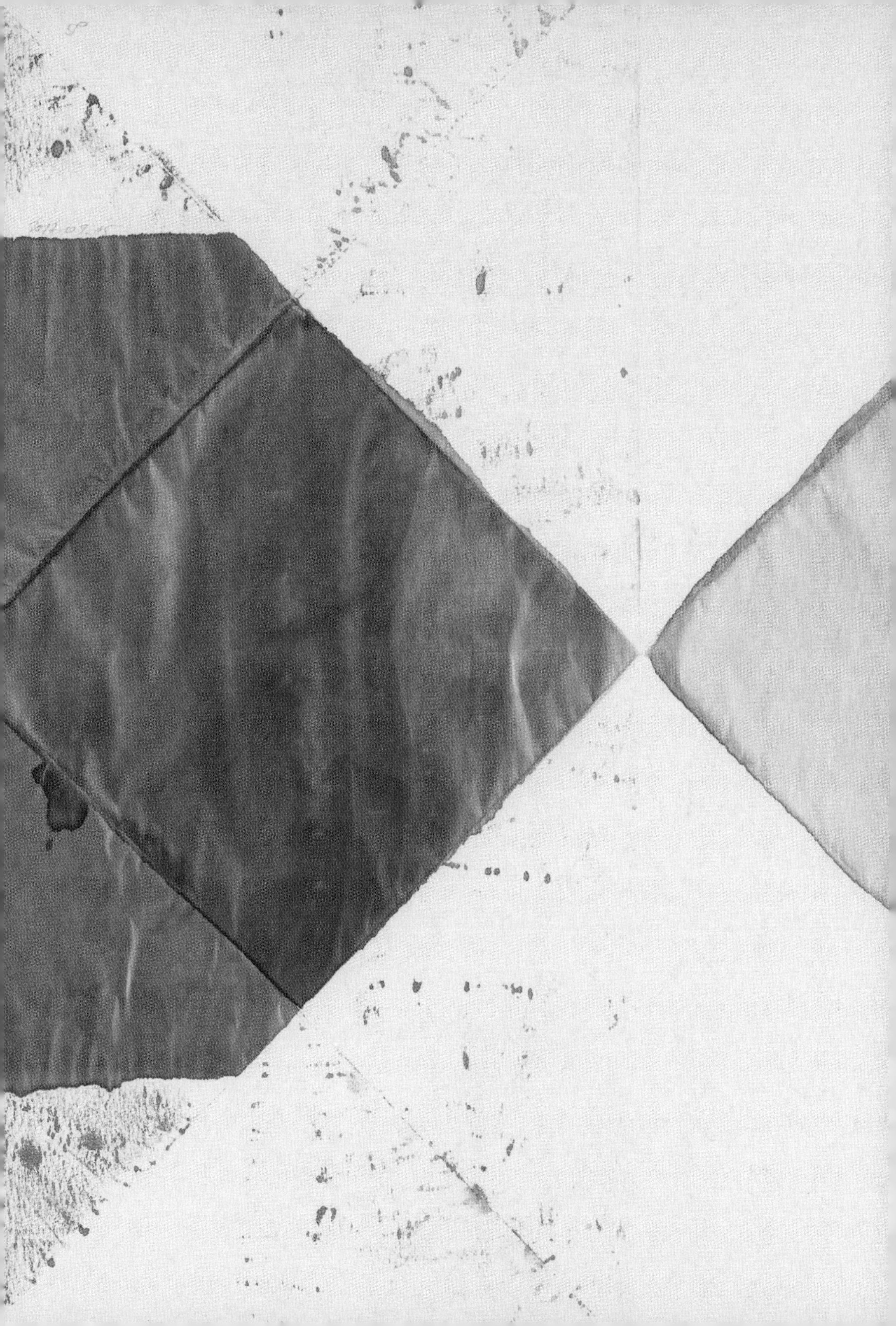

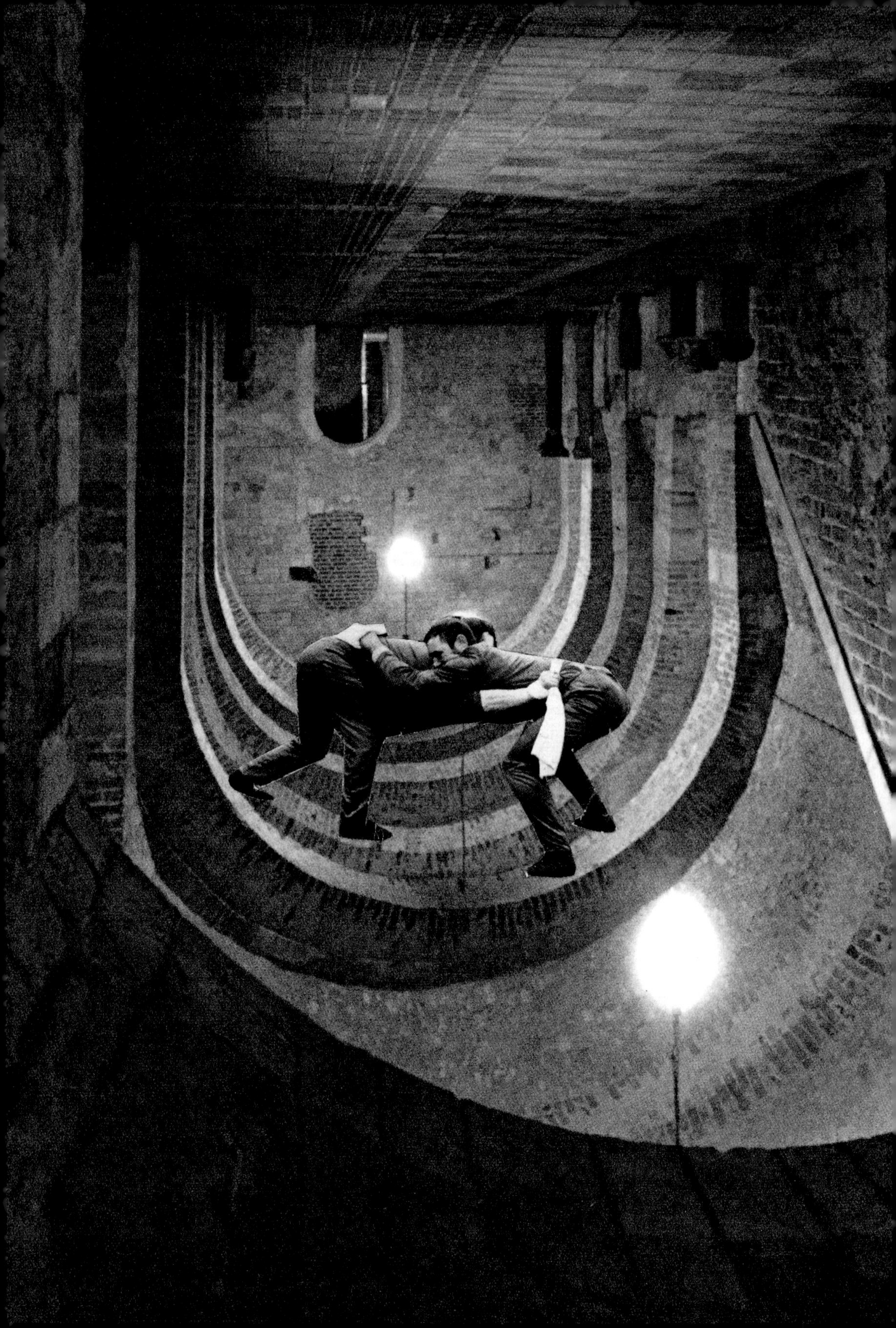

In the Beginning: A Transcript

Kim Schoen

In the beginning, there were certain wall panels that many
wanted to hang. Unfortunately there was not a consensus
that anyone was able to reach, and thus the foundation had
to be let go, and the beginning had to be found elsewhere.
When we start attempting to work by the book, people begin
to start with a medley of ideas — which means that no one
is in charge. When no one is in charge, things do begin
to disintegrate, so if you have the beginnings, as it
were, in the shade of a tree, not at the root of the tree,
what begins to happen is that something unravels… and in
the explication of the subject matter people begin to find
an uncommon clarity.

There is no mirror in which
anything can be reflected,
so when people look within
the family structure they
are considering whether
or not it is an option.
Another way to put it might
be to say that — with
today's technology — there
is no consensus.

There is a draping that
occurs in consciousness
when one is over-exercised
in reality. And in order
to escape that, there is a
trio, a medley as it were,
of ingredients that one can
incorporate, into the river
of thought. A 'what's for
dinner' kind of question
that takes it to the next
level… so that we're not
just a mere reflection in
the mirror anymore, we're
something new, something
without, and full of
possibility. There's a fear,
of course there's a fear
involved in such a decision.
Or maybe it's beyond
decision, beyond the power
of decision. Of course,
if it tastes right, do it.

Not that we're scholars, but it does bring to mind that
idea that we've skirted around and maybe that needs to
be discussed — not something definitive, laid down, like
the Declaration of Independence — but perhaps something
political, something political that you can grab onto,
and you can look forward to.

Zoe Kingsley

Moves Between Light

There is a man.

He only exists here.

He pivots towards the light, which comes through a window frame,
and then reverses his movement back to the shadows. With each turn
back he smiles and laughs.

We see him laugh, but we cannot hear it.
We have a side view of this man.
We are removed from what is happening as if in a dream.
We are watching a scene.

This man only exists here, but he once
existed in a dream, which happened
overnight sometime in March this year.

He is caught in between always.
He is mid-move ceaselessly.
He is a function, which doesn't extend beyond itself.
He is a machine.
He is a subversive machine; enacting malfunction within his function.
He is a cipher.

We feel implicated despite our removal.
We are dream-gazers.

Implication felt makes us feel illicit as subjects.
We become voyeurs.

Implication is infectious by its very nature of touching and connecting.
We can't discern between our illicitness and the object's potential for,
or actual being of, illicitness.

His being a subversive machine implicates illicit activity.

What is illicit sometimes is illicit by nature of its indeterminacy
and its suggestion of a possible impossible.

To feel is to recognise.

Illicitness felt is recognition of an unknown, to become known.

We have a self-knowledge.

Perversion is a moral subversion.
We have a perverse scene.

In her 1964 lecture 'On Classical Pornography', Susan Sontag claims an underlying connection between the comic and her definition of 'classical pornography'. According to Sontag, classical pornography doesn't necessarily involve the erotic, but alternatively concerns 'works of art which embody the idea that lascivious or lustful acts or thoughts are inherently immoral.' These critical embodiments can take the form of reflecting or transgressing a moralism essentialised in dominant representations of the sexual. In her lecture, Sontag draws a connection between comedy and the pornographic on the matters of form and content.

The form of classical pornography is parody, a sub-genre of comedy, which is reliant on quotation for effect. What may be limited within the illicit frame and framing of the illicit is in fact a grafting from the morally sanctioned and therefore is implicated with the sanctioned. This reaching and referencing beyond the frame is what produces laughter from the audience, a felt recognition of the unknown known.

What is felt through form is paradoxically undercut by content. The 'tremendous point of intersection between the spirit of comedy and consciousness that is expressed in [classical] pornography' according to Sontag, is the renouncement of feeling by characters within the narrative. This renouncement is twinned with neutralisation of affect, we as voyeurs are denied access to emotional depths and dimensionality. Characters are only 'instant'; they are rendered figures, 'ciphers' that operate on a suspended spatio-temporal plane. The dominant organisational principle of pornographic content is repetition: characters and implicated viewers continue in a state of incompletion, seeking gratification through consumption in inexhaustible revolutions. Ideals of progression and evolutionary movements into an alternative condition do not exist within the pornographic frame. These thematic concerns are explored within the 'stylised representations' of the real in tragedy according to Sontag. In the theatre of comedy and classical pornography, and one can argue, dreaming, what is left is a 'perpetual tableau': time and space represented through a singular performed repetition, torturous, rousing and never enough.

We make connections and seek causation so as to gain knowledge.
Knowledge gained or that which fails to be gained is self-knowledge.
It is a becoming.

This man who only exists here, his ceaseless pivots suggest a pattern.

A turn forward to the light, a turn back to the shadows.

His laugh corresponds with the turn back.

His laugh happens after a turn to the light.

His laugh is one of the cogs at work within the subversive machine.

We can interpret that the light causes the man to laugh.

We can interpret the light as a well-understood and accepted emblem of an elevated, formalised knowledge, a site of pedagogy.

We can interpret the man laughing after
turning to the light as the subversive machine
working through a received fault.

To function whilst malfunctioning.

We can argue that the man makes self-knowledge from
received elevated, formalised knowledge, from a site of
pedagogical exchange.

We can interpret self-knowledge as the negotiation in the
shadow, to laugh in the dark after receiving the faulty light.

The laugh is the convulsion,
    a flicker,
        a recurring glitch.

In the preface to the second edition of Aram
Saroyan's *Complete Minimal Poems*, Ron Silliman
frames Saroyan as a subversive 'miniaturist'
who 'took the heat'. His alleged subversiveness
epitomised cultural perversity within the arts
as defined by American Congress upon inclusion
of his one-word poem 'lighght' in *The American
Literary Anthology 2* in 1969, for which Saroyan
received National Endowment for the Arts
(NEA) money.

Saroyan's word-poems, such as 'lighght',
are re-presented ciphers within ciphers.
He demonstrates the innocence at work in the
unknown known and felt associations of words
experienced and applied in waking life, the
politics and humour of the pun. He makes
language a readymade image, extends language
beyond its primary function of descriptor or
metaphor. He reveals an ultimate paradox of
language, that of enacting a possible impossible,
to be both abstract and concrete.

Saroyan's 'lighght' unmasks a moral capital
intrinsic to the dominant and legitimised language
which circulates within a homogeneous politic,
the unacknowledged bias which dictates what is
acceptable and accepted. Saroyan illustrates that

to make 'lighght' of the Institution is not just a
subversive act but a perversity condemnable by
higher authorities. For to make a joke of language
is to destabilise normalised sense-making, to
threaten existent power structures. To laughgh
is to actually *see* the malfunction within the func-
tioning machine, the instability in the flickering
light of sanctioned knowledges and pedagogies.

In my dream existence today I finish a half-day's
work late and go to the Institution's library to
return films. I pick up a photography book on
sale, an object of obscura: a thin paperback
catalogue of an exhibition in Cardiff from 2000
titled *Journeys in the Dreamland*, which features
work from three contemporary Australian photographers. I flick through, pages repetitious with
images. 'a n n e z a h a l k a' appears justified
centre beneath the title 'F O R T R E S S E S
& F R O N T I E R S'. The photos which follow
have been made into light boxes, an advertising
medium as noted by curator Christopher
Coppock in the introduction to the catalogue.

In his introduction to *Journeys in the Dreamland*,
Coppock confesses to the reader of his
preconceptions of the Australian outback as
a foreigner, a Northern Irish foreigner with

'anti-imperialist sentiments' who, despite his politics, nevertheless cannot help sate a 'touristic fascination for a silver-screen mediated landscape'. His fascination motivates an expedition, so to speak, into rural NSW. His self-re-defined position post-NSW-expedition 'is where *Journeys in the Dreamland* emerged', an attempt to represent experience of an (enlightened) ambivalence towards the subject of Australia through curatorship and book-object. The success of this is debatable, given that attempts to represent easily become complicit within the operations of colonialism. This is arguably the case here given the lack of diversity of the artists chosen. All three photographers are white, at least two of the three are second generation Australians with European heritage, but no photographers from diasporas outside of Europe, or from Aboriginal and Torres Strait Islander communities are included. Where Coppock the curator tries and misses the mark, Zahalka the photographer doesn't. Maybe this is where image manages to supersede written self-analysis. Coppock's study of Zahalka's photographs engages with the lure and conceit of the frame, that is, of Zahalka's resistance towards a dominant narrative and representative character. People within the cityscape are mere 'material presence[…] [t]he

citizen becomes an inanimate object'. This is the condition of Zahalka's perpetual tableau.

And how the light features in these images is remarkable.

As someone who was born in Melbourne, but whose associations with place of birth are of temporal and imaginative distance, informed by a tricksy two-fold nostalgia developed from living outside of the country once as a child and presently as an adult, it is a feel for these constructed jade-lit urban spaces, the heat of these urban spaces, which render other Western empire-building notions of New World metropolis inapplicable.

The light and the heat seen is lurid and dripping and bleached and chlorinated and salty, and the city which is revealed is a picture of (commercial) imperialism. A colonisation of space which is ubiquitous, and a decay forcefully sustained, a cultural corrosive.

These photos were taken of Sydney's cityscape in 1993, the year of my birth, and the photographer at the time of these images would have been the same age as my mother that very year.

According to Simone Weil's definition of gravity in *Gravity and Grace*, gravity is a kind of secular journey, a navigation of what is received, a negotiation of, for lack of better terms, good and evil. It is a process of creation from base materials of environment, 'roots' and traditions, which has the potential for corruption. Gravity is a force that 'rule[s] the universe.' Another force, which rules alongside gravity, is light.

For the man who only exists here, each bodily retraction can be interpreted as folding into the self. That is, to negotiate a positioning of self in relation to the originary fold, which is ceaselessly returned to within the scene, a scene which continues to play.

Light is important in Glasgow where dreaming now takes place.
Light tricks, it drags and time seemingly stalls with its delay.

I saw the light and felt its heat in the last weekend of
March, boarding a suburban train Southside, not my
typical line but an adjacent one. It felt like a dream.

It is a Mother's Day Sunday and the clocks have just been moved
forward. I walk the blocks to the Centre of Contemporary Art
to watch a film featuring in the GLITCH Film Festival before
making my way down to Central Station to meet a friend. We sit
in the concrete Cloister Garden of St Andrew's Cathedral by the
River Clyde, the sun refracting off the mirrored plinth memorials.
We then grab pints at the nearby Clutha Bar. Sweating, we board
the train back southbound.

In an almost empathic synchronicity with the object of our gaze,
the scene witnessed brightens and fades with each repetition, with
each pivot by the man who only exists here.

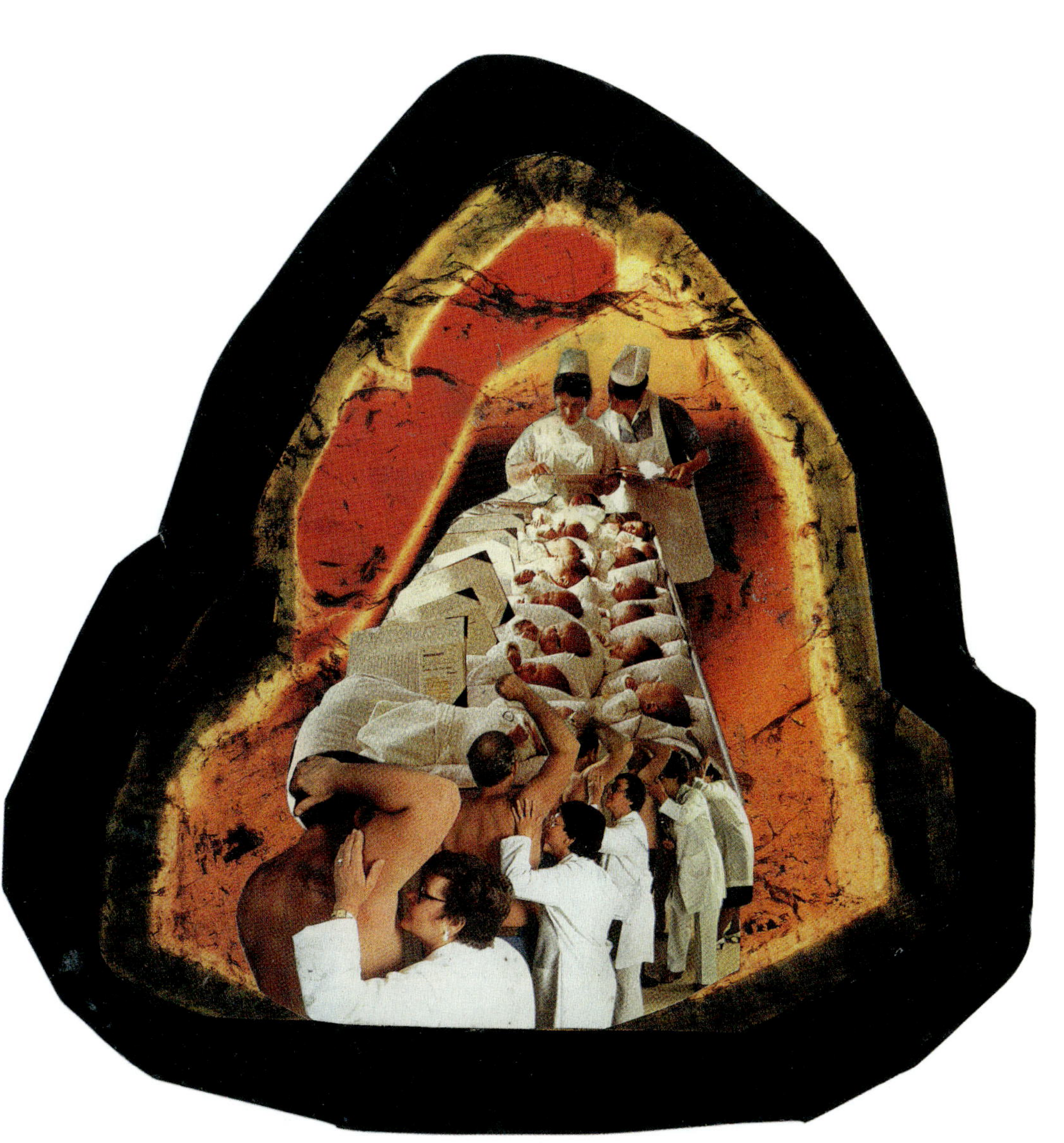

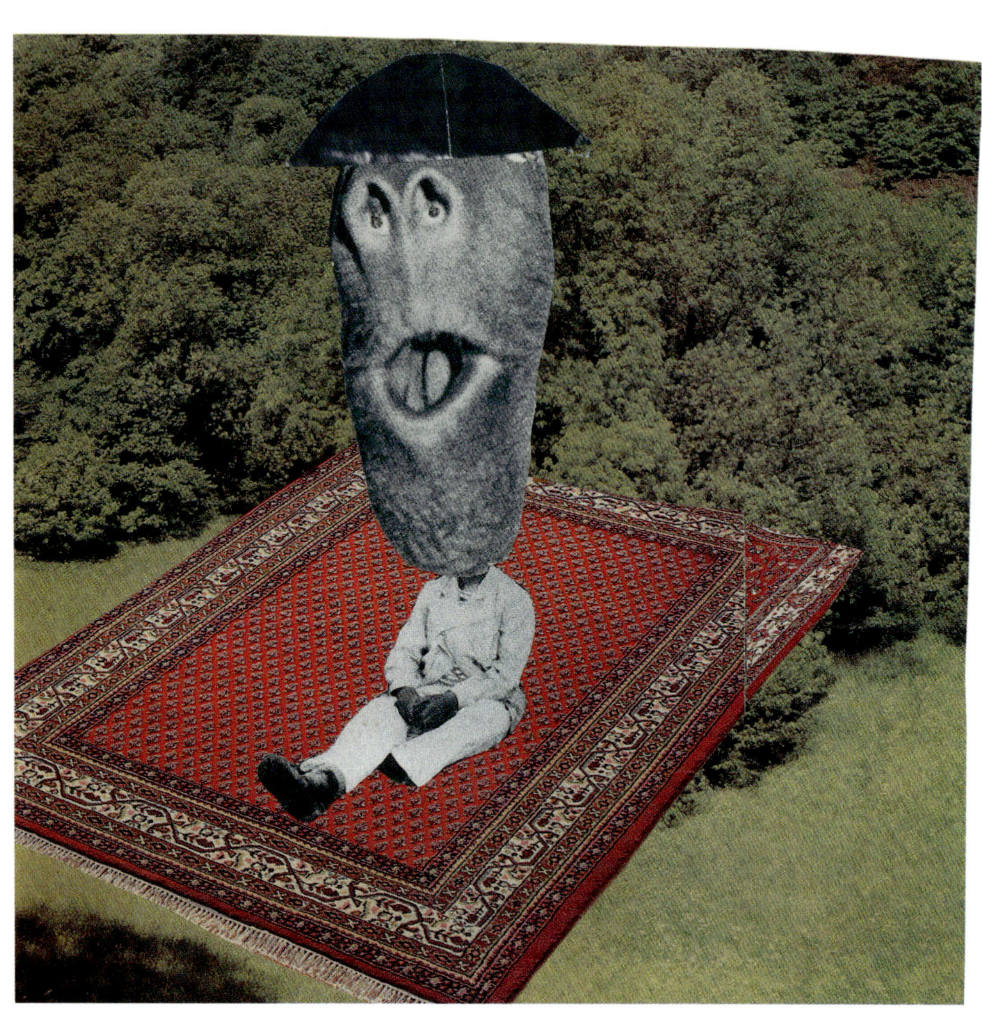

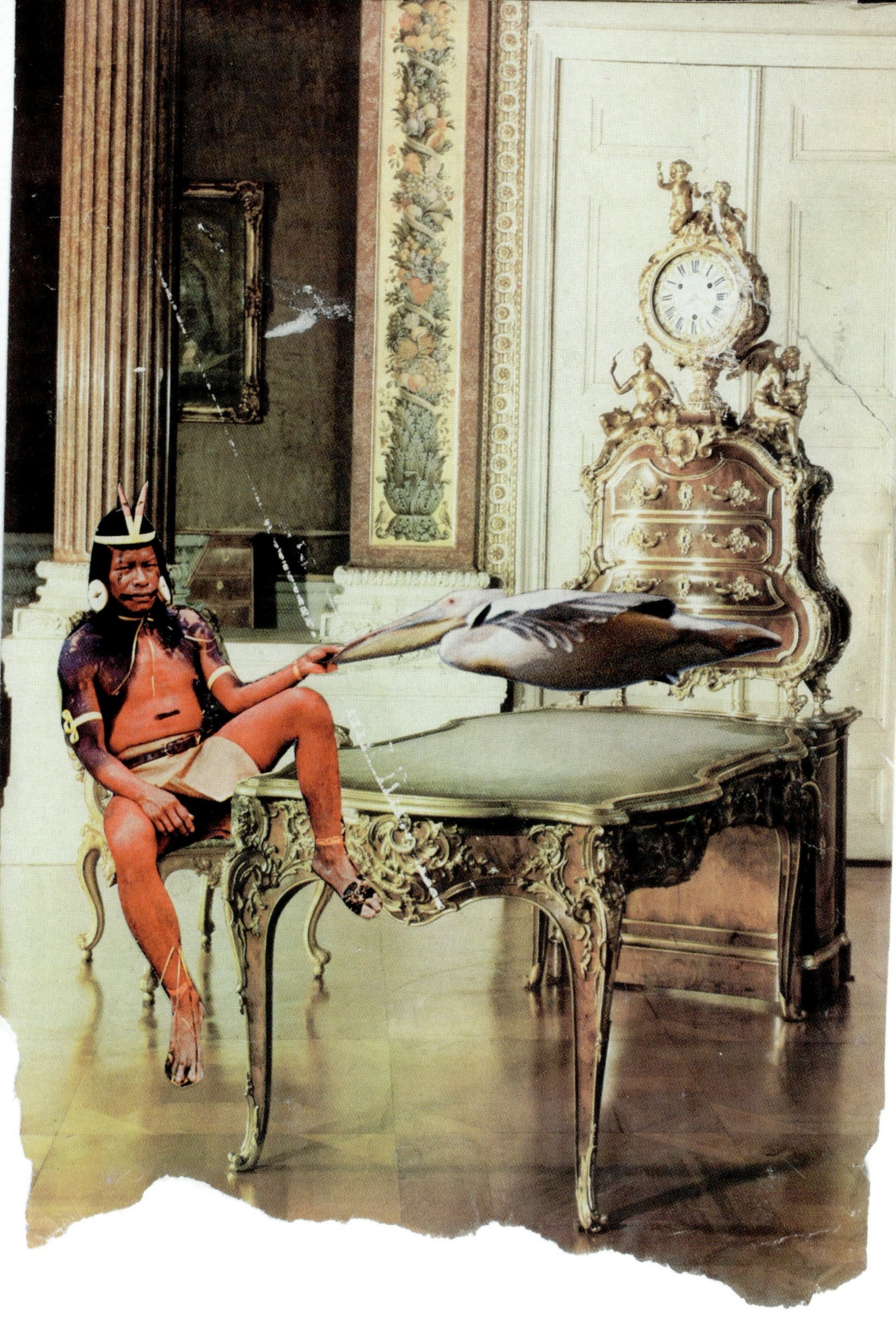

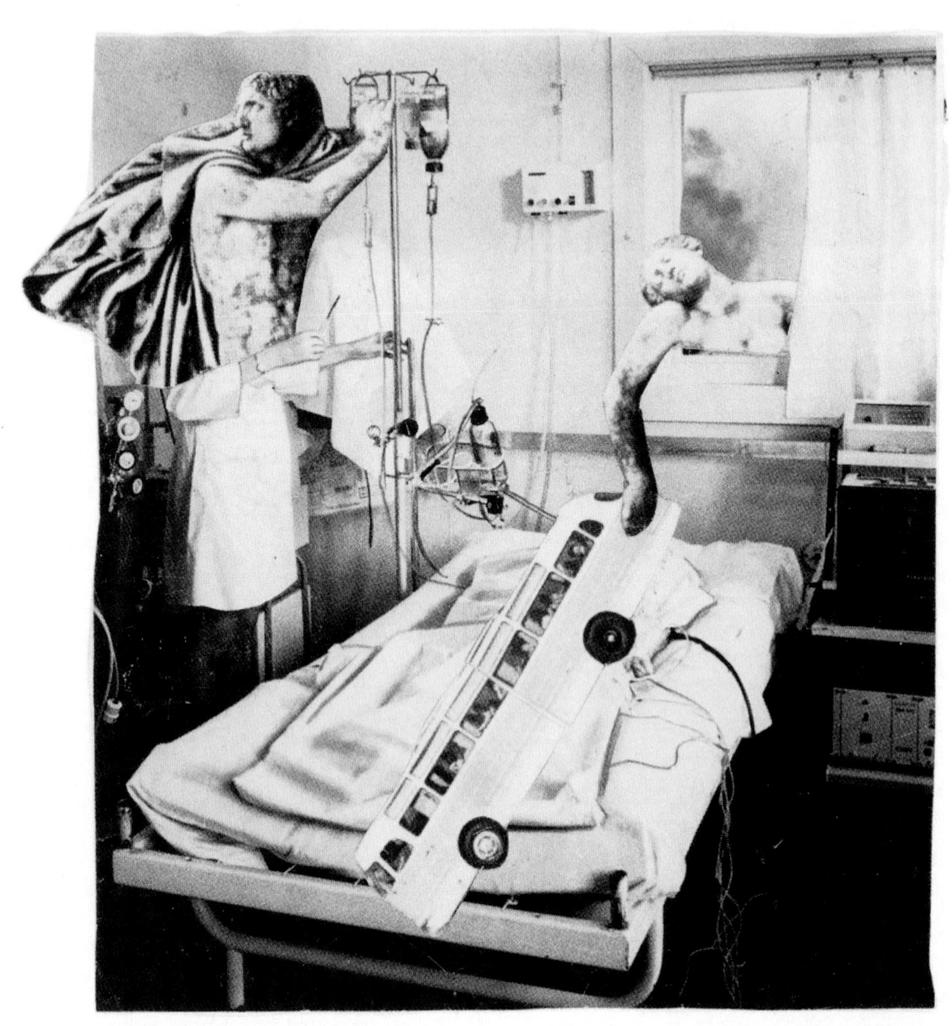

MORTA DELLA

MICHAEL LAWTON

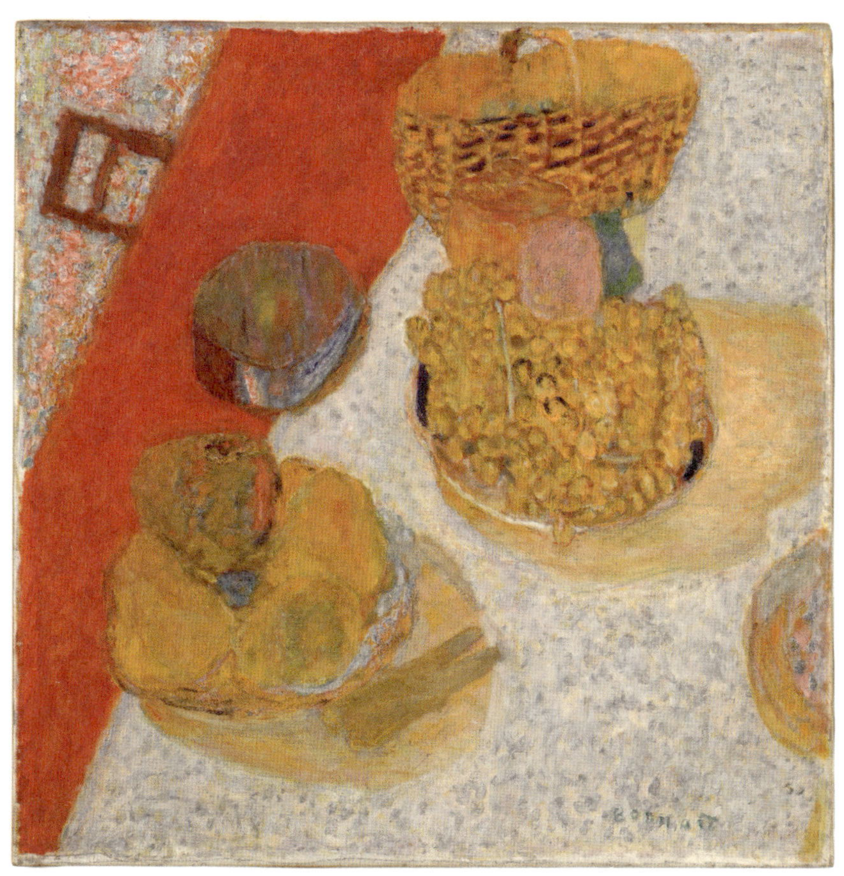

When Arabella Carter was very young she was
already the best in the town at naming things.

Shilick she said, four years old and pointing at the
damp grass that seemed always damp, drooping
like towel-dried hair toward the cracks in the
pavement, and soon everyone in our constituency
was calling it Shilick Grass.

She was twenty-one when she named the blue-
black birds that feed on the Shilick, Torozens.
It was actually from their habit of eating facing
the horizon, she told me one day in my studio,
that she drew inspiration for their name.
But to those who didn't know, there was simply
some Torozen-ness about these birds and
their patient stance, some Torozen-ness about
the Torozens that we were now all aware of.

She called the fall you have as you are dropping
off to sleep, the Thistimble.

She called the moment of being frozen with fear
when you wake from a nightmare Garllantheon.

She called the sensation on the tongue as it sucks
back between the pebbles, Shishingle.

It was impossible not to see our constituency, our
world, through her words, from the Bartomollotas
grazing in our fields to the Palmillo tree, the fruits
of which, the Palmilla, we eat every summer.

Chips of paint she called Tecks.

The unsure footing of shoes on artificial turf
she called Fwooth.

The tearing of one's jealous heart she
called Wriwrac.

She named all our colours. When I travelled,
I realised that we don't all think colours the same
way; the painter might think in terms of weight,
the cook might give colours flavours, the iconoclast,
fury, but in our town we had all learnt to think
of colours as Arabella did. Diozomi was the blue
of the evening sky in April, Pulmaca the purple of

Bartomollota shit. The colour of the blood of the
trees she called Dinzengent, and then we would
call anything else of that tawny red Dinzengent,
and we also used it as an adjective to describe
fertility and harvest time. Her words were fuzzed
sometimes through our usage but they still had
their roots in her.

The ink stains she got on her fingers after writing
she called Falruises and all of us called the ink
stains we got on our fingers after writing Falruises.

The sucking wince she made when her mother
applied iodine to her scraped knees she called
Cha and then all of us called the sucking wince
we made when our mothers applied iodine to our
scraped knees Cha.

The mild flashbacks to hallucinations that
were neither blissful nor terrifying, she called
Polzetos and all of us called the mild flashbacks
to hallucinations that were neither blissful nor
terrifying, Polzetos.

This skill of appositeness of description, this
appropriateness of her word skills, resulted in
many of her neighbours, my countrymen, applying
to her for advice on other matters. At first she'd
respond, flattered and demure; demurring
'I am a poet not a doctor' or 'I am a poet not
a sorceress.' And it is true that back then she was
more reticent about naming for others, about
giving out advice, about settling disputes, about
rebranding the rundown.

'What of the old names?' she said, 'what will
become of them?'

There was some truth in this. Some of the
creatures lost their edges after being embraced
by her vocabulary, lost that which wasn't captured
by her names: The feathers of the Kooxans lost
their eyes, or these eyes lost the ability of sight
anyway, became nothing more than glassy lolling
spheres; delicious when fried, crispy on the outside,
runny inside. After all it was also true that the
Kooxans were a lot easier to catch once their
panoptic vision had gone.

Sometimes she would suggest names for children of kin; she told me what I would name my daughter, and I did, but she went no further than that in her advice.

We all see the world through our own eyes. But I remember thinking that for her it must have been different. The world came to meet her eyes, it must have felt to her that the world almost wanted to be seen the way she saw it. Unlike me she never left, and her words became embedded in everything, little by little she bleached all her surroundings until her world was as she wished it.

I don't know if this is why but at some point she changed her mind on offering advice, on getting involved in the lives of others, perhaps she wanted their worlds to look more like hers. At this point I was travelling outside the city at the end of my youth, on national service, but before I left, word of her ability was spreading beyond our constituency. This would have been the end of her youth too. When I returned not only was she dispensing advice more readily, she had also made some powerful friends.

I can't really dilk or complain; I took her moffer too, when she was in my studio that day she bought a painting I'd made of the moon. She told me I should only make paintings of the moon, and I did, and made my name as an artist.

She came to know a businessman TH Lavinder and with her help, naming each of his franchises differently, he became very rich. He seemed to have amassed his fortune whilst I was away, there was a park that was renamed Lavindery before I left, because of the lavender that grew there, or so Arabella said. In my absence Lavinder had taken ownership of it, it was in his name after all, and he levelled the park and built flats, expanding into property.

When TH Lavinder decided he wanted to run for mayor, Arabella was involved in his electioneering; everyone said that her provision of a name – Remuner & Remuner – to his particular, radical wealth redistribution-solution for austerity, was the reason for its popularity.

During his candidacy she helped expose the nepotism that the incumbent mayor profited from by naming it Chachality. Until it was named we weren't able to see how septic, rife and damaging it was, both to democracy and to the way we were perceived outside of our country. As the bodies of the now former mayor and his deputy were left in a tank in the main square she called the process of their putrefaction Sanstein.

The aqueduct that marked the beginning of Lavinder's ambitions for expansion, she called Forevet. The water that flooded the fields after the rains, diverted there by Forevet, she called Tillender. Dinzengent was buxful because of Tillender for a whole vicade and the city got wealthier and wealthier.

Soon more and more of her words had entered our vocabulary. Was she speaking for Lavinder or he for her? When he came onto the delepatheron and said Asturton! Asturton Piatges! We weren't really that surprised.

When we went to war she called the machines our soldiers rode off in Coupaers, and she blessed them.

She called the blood of our enemies, Dismalaplay.

The children of our enemies, Jattle.

The name of their land, Dogerer.

Jonas Žakaitis

The Oldest Woman

'I met the oldest woman in the world today.'

'How old?'

'122.'

'122?'

'Yeah. Someone even made a football shirt for her, with a number 122 and some company logos on it, a smiling envelope on the front and a globe on the back. It's her birthday today.'

'Did the news desk send you?'

'Yeah. Quite a few journalists were invited to that retirement home. We drank champagne and ate cake. Guess what the most popular question was?'

'Secrets of longevity?'

'Mhm. Everyone talked about the same thing, but the old lady didn't talk much. Her consciousness was like a lighthouse, it seemed, turning towards you for a few seconds, shining on you, then turning away to somewhere else. Sometimes even in the middle of a sentence you could feel her leaving words on their own and wandering off.'

'Just think about it, she was born in the nineteenth century.'

'Nurses cleaned her room so well that everything seemed untouched, no fingerprints anywhere. There wasn't a single thing on her bedside table, not even a glass of water. Her pyjamas and all the bed linen were brand new. The old lady was bathed so well that even the smell of old age had gone.'

'I wonder what was she doing when she was our age?'

'Her body seemed to be subject to fourfold gravity. All the people and the furniture are rising slowly around her, but she is sliding downwards. Everything is sterilised and because of that there is no sound, like in mime. Can you imagine?'

'But think about it, when she was a teenager…'

'Yeah, cars looked like carriages, people sent telegrams and thought that war was a matter of honour.'

'Mhm.'

'I've tried to find something out about her life, but without success. The Institute of Gerontology found three documents with her surname, but it was slightly different in each of them. It seems that she was born in Ukraine and sixty years ago she lived in France. No one at the retirement home remembers who brought her and no one found any papers.'

'Didn't you ask her?'

'I tried. She smiled back.'

'Didn't say anything?'

'Told everyone to help themselves to more cake.'

'What else?'

'Nothing. Whenever the lighthouse turned towards us – just offering cake, smiling and repeating that she is very old and we are all very young.'

'Mhm. Which is true by the way.'

'And whenever it turned away, murmuring something incomprehensible. Later they sat her up in bed and wrapped her in a blanket.'

'Did you stay there for long?'

'No, everyone started leaving, but I kept on staring at her hands. Do you know what the hands of a very old person look like?'

'Like a turtle.'

'Maybe more like crumpled baking paper. Not only wrinkled, but also a bit shiny. I don't know why.'

'Mhm.'

'We were alone. She sat and looked at me without moving once. When everybody left, the lighthouse slowed down even more. Sometimes she gave me that look as if she recognised somebody in my face, and then drifted away again. I pulled my chair closer to her bed and gripped her hands.'

'What?'

'As tightly as I could, almost. She didn't shout, she didn't do anything. She'll recognise me in a bit, I thought, or she'll get scared, but no. She looks straight at me, but I remind her of too many things. Too many similar occurrences.'

(But of course we know it wasn't anything like that. Nurses rushed into
the ward with unopened champagne bottles, and dresses. You wanted
to try them all on. This one reminds me of Paris, you said, that's when
I tried that knee-length dress with the chiffon petticoat for the first time.
I'm getting old too, I want to tell you this, but can't find the words. Saying
that I'm getting old now sounds as useless as saying that I'm scared of
the atomic bomb. By the way, what did you feel when you found out
that the atomic bomb had just exploded? Did all the people in the world
put their tools slowly on the ground that same minute and realise for a
moment that going to work, keeping all your promises or knowing which
way is North hasn't changed a thing? Yeah, you laugh, this moment
should be the theme for our party. I watch the nurses taking off their
uniforms, giggling, touching each other's thighs and slipping into glossy
dresses. Wait, there's something else I want to ask! I've already called
a cab, you say, and you haven't changed yet. I can't come up with a
question that's worthy of you, I complain. But there is no holding back,
the nurses burst out of the ward, and fly through the corridors, jostling
and racing down the stairs.)

Restaurant Sankt Peterburgas

Jonas Žakaitis

You laugh because I'm only thirteen and I am already at the table wearing a jacket and trying to order some vodka. (Because there is nothing else to drink here, only vodka on the menu.) I saw everything, you came in thick black coats and knee-high snowy boots. I saw colourful sweaters under your coats, with tigers and panthers, and waterfalls and jungle birds. Then I saw you quickly taking those snowy boots off, sticking them into plastic bags and hiding them under the table, and slipping into those high heels you had brought on the sly. Where are your husbands? Why didn't they come tonight? (Actually I know, I saw them standing at the taxi stop in leather jackets that you chose for them. They were arranging payments for the sauna. I know what they're up to. I often meet them. When someone bought a remote-controlled lawn mower, they were standing around it for a long time, everybody wanting to run it and unable to sort out whose turn it was.) Look at that boy sitting there, such a serious face, better come dance with us, you say loudly and pull my arms. I'm shy, because I don't know how to dance, so I force myself to take another sip of vodka. But you know how to dance and sing. You know how to cook stews with bay leaves and make jams, and you know how to choose the right watermelon, and how to stuff shoes with newspapers to dry them. You cry as soon as it gets sad, and then you call each other and talk over the phone for a very long time. And not only can I not find the words, I'm also sitting here alone and suffering with this vodka. Come on, enough sitting, you tell me. I try not to look at your bodies, at those stupendous breasts underneath those tigers. But you are lifting skirts, and twisting your thighs, on purpose, and then checking your hair with the palms of your hands. You clap and laugh when I climb onto the table to give a speech. I don't know what is loosening my tongue, but I promise to hire a bus next week, collect you all, and drive around for the whole day. I would like to go shopping with you all, for fabrics and carpets, I say. You will keep on dancing and singing, unwrapping all the rolls of fabric and cutting off as much as you want. And then we will fill the whole bus with those fabrics. Write down your phone numbers for me, I say, I'll call you.

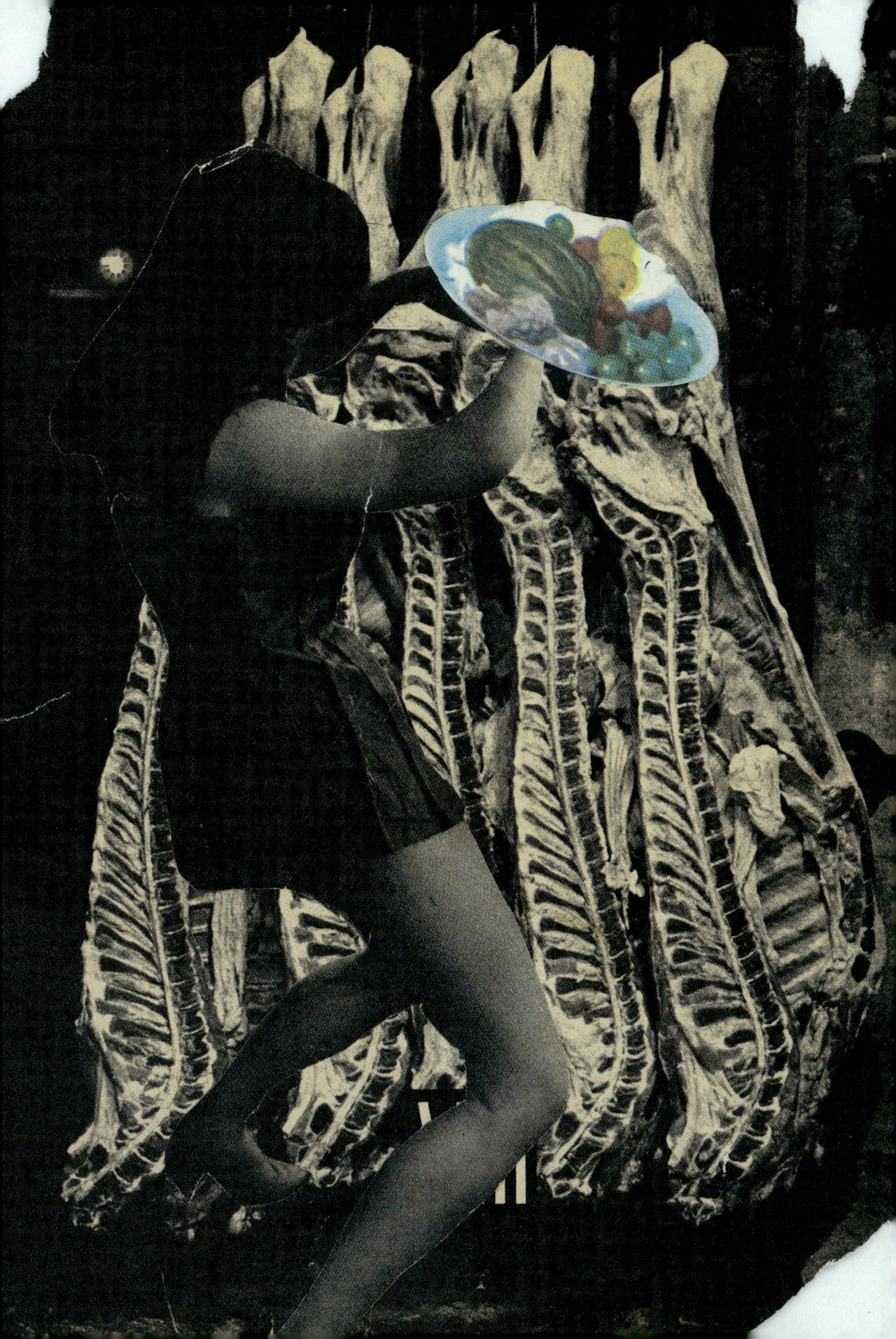

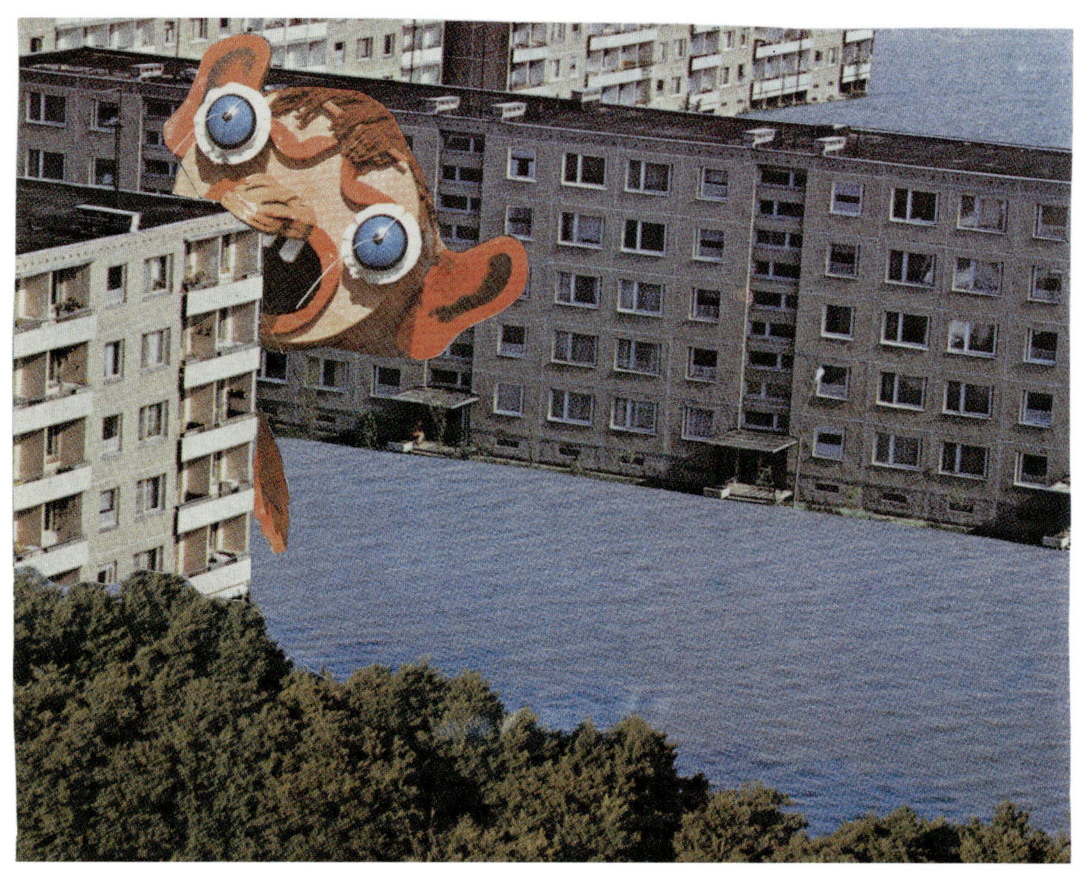

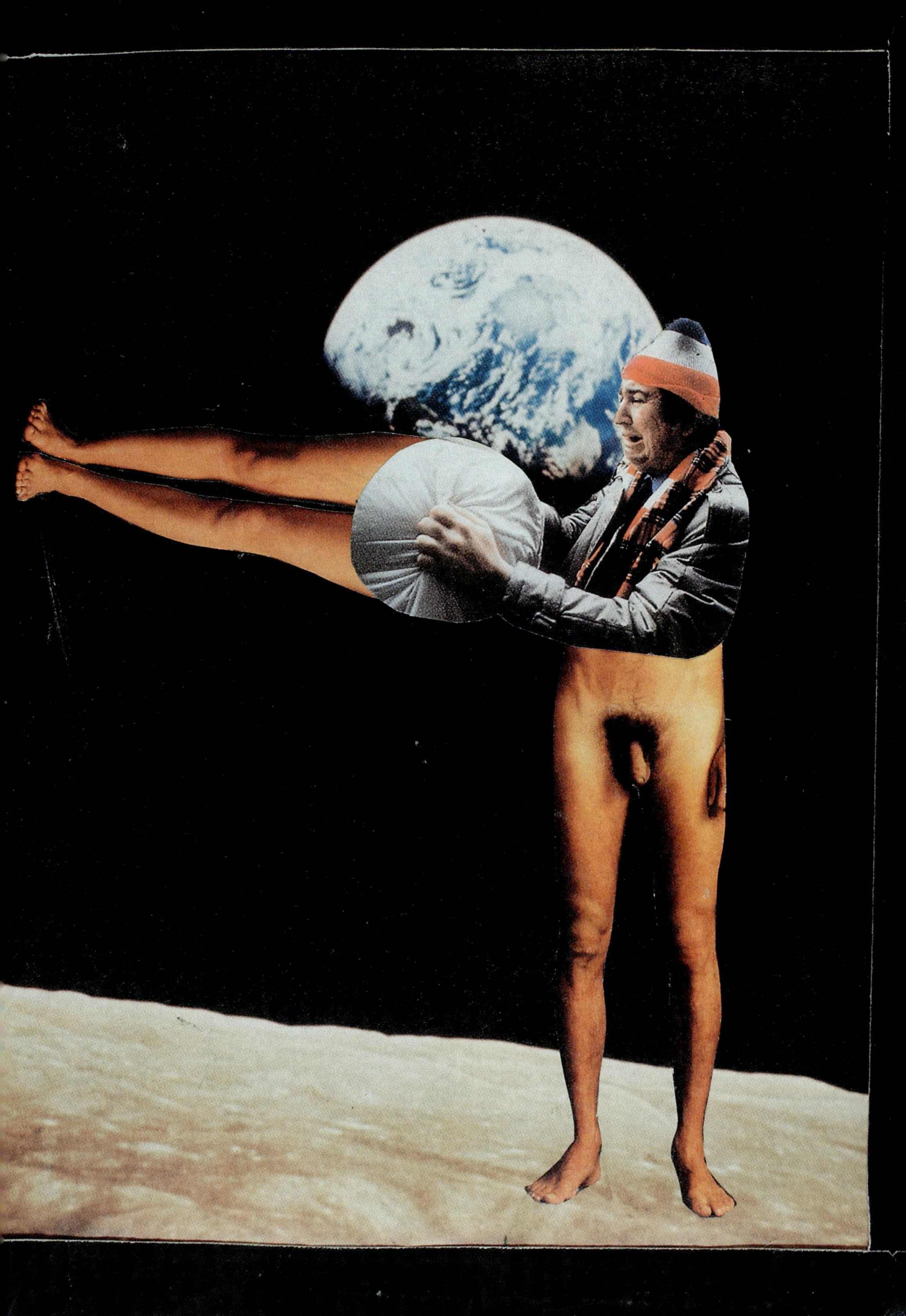

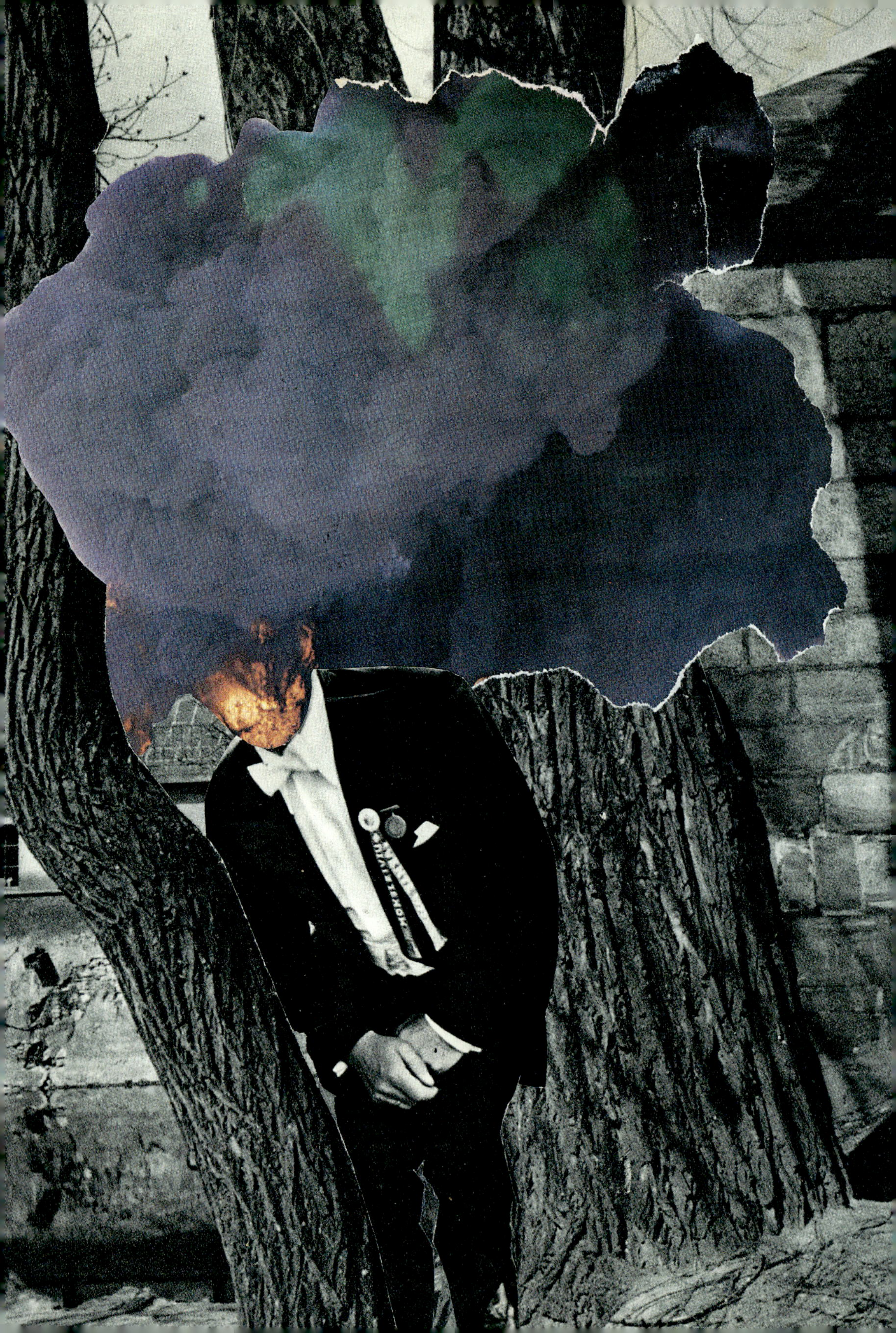

Cemetery Detective

Monika Kalinauskaitė

Before talking about anything else, I think we should talk
about my aunt. She is so funny, I'm telling you, although
it's obviously a bit sad that she's so lonely. My aunt also
lives in one of the residential districts, you know, in
the tower block. Her wallpaper is so funny, I can't even…
My grandma had a similar one with tulips of some kind, and
moons. Bonkers, I'm telling you.

So yeah, the interesting thing is that my aunt is a cemetery
detective. Yes yes, I didn't get it either at first. It
seemed a bizarre joke, too much fantasising. But she didn't
make it up by herself, you know, she got hired by the local
council, and the chair of residents is very happy to have
such a detective. Anyway, what does she do? She goes to
that cemetery all the time, every weekend — there is mum,
grandma, also a few neighbours, everyone pretty much.
She always notices and talks about whose grave is being
well looked after, what kind of flowers are around and where,
which ones were probably put there by a daughter, which
graves are never visited anymore and just get candles
lit on the All Saints' Day. She investigated a couple of
small crimes. It turns out that someone was doing a bit
of smuggling. She found a foreign tax stamp near the
grandma's, and the lawn was seeming very Belarusian somehow.
The customs office even sent her a letter of appreciation.
So then, thanks to neighbours of neighbours, she got famous.
Every weekend, after visiting the cemetery, she goes to the
police station where an officer writes down her report and
then they continue the investigation from there. You know,
there's so much mafia around these days — they put soil mixed
with salt on graves, and there's a black market for marble,
forged crosses, candles with sleeping gas, shovels stolen
and resold… And now in this way she even adds a couple of

pennies to her salary. Because she is actually a teacher.
I have no idea how she still gets anything across to
the kids. Her voice is strained, but when she talks
about that cemetery it becomes quieter at once, softer.
Perhaps she calms down.

And you know, I was thinking to myself — that aunt of mine
is a woman after all. Although she never got married, she
still looks after herself, puts some makeup on. Mum used
to say that I was a bit vainglorious, but how much can
one do in that room? I don't know, maybe it's different
for you, but it's only fun to be in front of the computer
or the mirror at my place. I was trying to move, stretch
my legs, I can almost do the splits. I did origami some
time ago, but all the cranes flew away through the open
window, and once you fly out, you can only climb around
at the playground with children, or run breathless.
A strange world anyway. You know, I buy flowers for myself
in the supermarket sometimes, especially tulips. So then
you take one like a microphone, sing something, like
in your childhood days, and it almost seems that the tulip
talks back to you. It opens up slightly and a kind of
moaning comes from there, a small beetle comes out and
then lives with you… Ok, I know, I know, a dreamer, talking
nonsense. But really, how much can one do in that room
or that district?

RAUSCHENBERG & BREXIT ARE BRAVING THE SURF

ISABEL WAIDNER

We have fighter planes rockets explosions on our sweaters this is not Top Gun this is not an haute couture fashion show. This is the Isle of Wight off the south coast of England, the beach outside Ryde. Giorgiy is wearing their military green parka over their sweater it's parka weather in June. Black oversize joggers, white Reebok classic trainers. 'The pronoun is "they",' Giorgiy signals. 'Ok', I reply. The Isle of Wight (IoW) is home to the British space rocket industry, and Her Majesty's IoW high security prison complex. British beaches. Giorgiy is looking for their parent, apparently. Their mother, their father, it's all relative. As far as Giorgiy can tell, their parent is not on the beach. 'What about this one', I ask. No. Negative. Giorgiy thinks that their parent is more likely to reside in Her Majesty's prison complex (HMP Parkhurst) than on the beach. Why do you say that, I ask. Giorgiy doesn't say. Giorgiy and I are new to the Isle of Wight. We are second and first generation migrants from Golders Green, North West London. We are pacifists and we have tanks on our sweaters (the times we live in). Robert Rauschenberg's *Mud Muse* (1968–71) is a 12ft by 9ft glass and aluminium tank with bubbling bentonite clay inside. The tank is equipped with microphones and a tape machine recording the bubbling, which in turn (in play mode) triggers a system of pumps inciting new bentonite (Benny) activity. Rauschenberg's piece is in a museum in London what's it got to do with Isle of Wight beach life. The tide is low the ground is wet the terrain is launching bentonite missiles, that's what. The local MP is delighted with the EU referendum result the Isle of Wight voted 61.95% in favour of leaving the European Union. ('We have done it (voted to Leave), and that is all we can do.') Bullet rain from the terrain upwards is this a natural event or national politics. WHAM! BAM! A projectile hits Giorgiy on the shoulder. We retaliate FIGHTER PLANES ROCKETS EXPLOSIONS ARE GOING OFF THEY REALLY ARE GOING OFF NOW WE ARE NOT WEARING OUR SWEATERS FOR NO REASON. As if connected via a hidden tape machine, Benny activity on the ground is increasing proportionally. 'Over there', I say. 'Is it your parent?' Stuck in a black and white car tyre, Rauschenberg's taxidermied merino sheep (*Monogram*, 1955–59), like us, is dodging bentonite bullets. Giorgiy isn't sure about this one they are going to have to take a closer look. On inspection, *Monogram* ('Money') is reminding Giorgiy not of their parent, but the IoW's Brexit-done Brexit-doing MP. The way it's stuck in its black and white tyre. 'But Giorgiy', I say. 'It's got rainbow coloured acrylics all over its face.' 'Still', Giorgiy says. Rainbow flag or not, they aren't convinced of its pro-European orientation. They think we might be dealing with a representative of the UKIP or English Defense League LGBTQI divisions. The rise of the UKIP or English Defense League LGBTQI divisions is not a joke it is very serious. Giorgiy thinks we should leave Money on the beach where we found it on the grounds of its potential links to right wing LGBTQI organisations. Giorgiy would rather be safe than sorry. Benny missiles are flying they are airborne like starlings I've hated the intimation of paintballing from the beginning. WHAMBAM! Another hit, echoing Giorgiy's T-shirt with the pink-mouthed shark, b&w stripy flashes, and blood dripping from the hem upwards. WHAMBAM! it says on said T-shirt which Giorgiy isn't wearing not under their sweater and never with their black oversize joggers. The pink-mouthed shark rises from the sea surfing a tidal wave, what if this part of the beach were about to get flooded. This isn't a haute couture fashion show and this isn't a surfer's paradise. Already the water is rising our Reeboks are drenched. 'Let's go', I say. Giorgiy just wants to make sure their parent isn't over there. The pink-mouthed shark releases a b&w stripy lightning bolt from its eye. The lightning bolt travels across the left hand side of the T-shirt including the sleeve, creating a zebraesque dreamworld. 'It's raining, Giorgiy', I say. But Giorgiy will not be slowed down by the rain this is England Giorgiy is British (second gen). In the 1950s and '60s, the short-lived British space rocket programme saw the IoW's Needles Headland transformed into a real-life double-0 seven film. British space rockets were assembled in underground workshops, apparently, then launched into the atmosphere from the Needles rocket-testing site (like fireworks). I want an astronaut who is not Tim Peake (I want Mae Jemison, or Helen Sharman). On the Esplanade, a demonstration is building momentum. Local party activists are flying the rainbow flag. Amongst the demonstrators is Giorgiy's parent (?), carrying a placard: 'Some gays vote UKIP. Get over it.' 'Don't let homophobic bigots enter our country.' 'Britain First!' Giorgiy doesn't smile I don't smile we are migrants from north-west London. We roll out the tanks on our sweaters and make straight for the Esplanade. What if the earth were riddled with microphones. What if a tape machine were recording the tracks of our tanks, what if (on playback) a hole opened up under the Esplanade and swallowed the demonstration. What if a pink-mouthed shark rode in on a tidal wave, what if a b&w lightning bolt from its eye turned the scene into a zebraesque fantasy. But this isn't an art installation this isn't a motif on a designer t-shirt. This is the Isle of Wight off the south coast of England. This is what we are faced with.

SHOOTING STARS

DAVID BERNSTEIN

I can see a wild Texas cowboy teacher pointing his gun at the blackboard beginning to lecture. The board is covered in white stars and the table in front of him is full of planetary models. His other hand, holding a second gun, is pointing at the models while he tells the class about intergalactic dimensions. The scene is an astronomy lesson in a strange and paranoid world.

The absurdity of this image starts to take shape in my mind in a conversation at my parents' synagogue. This old woman with an oxygen mask next to her armchair tells me it's a good thing that almost all Texans are armed with guns, because then ISIS won't mess with us. Not only does this seem like an extremely violent contradiction coming from a soft-spoken disabled woman, but she proudly continues to inform me about a new law going into effect in Texas where anyone can openly carry a gun into any public building, including universities. This means that a classmate sitting next to you can have a gun hanging off their belt. This means that a teacher can stand in front of a classroom pointing at the blackboard with a gun in his or her hand instead of a piece of chalk.

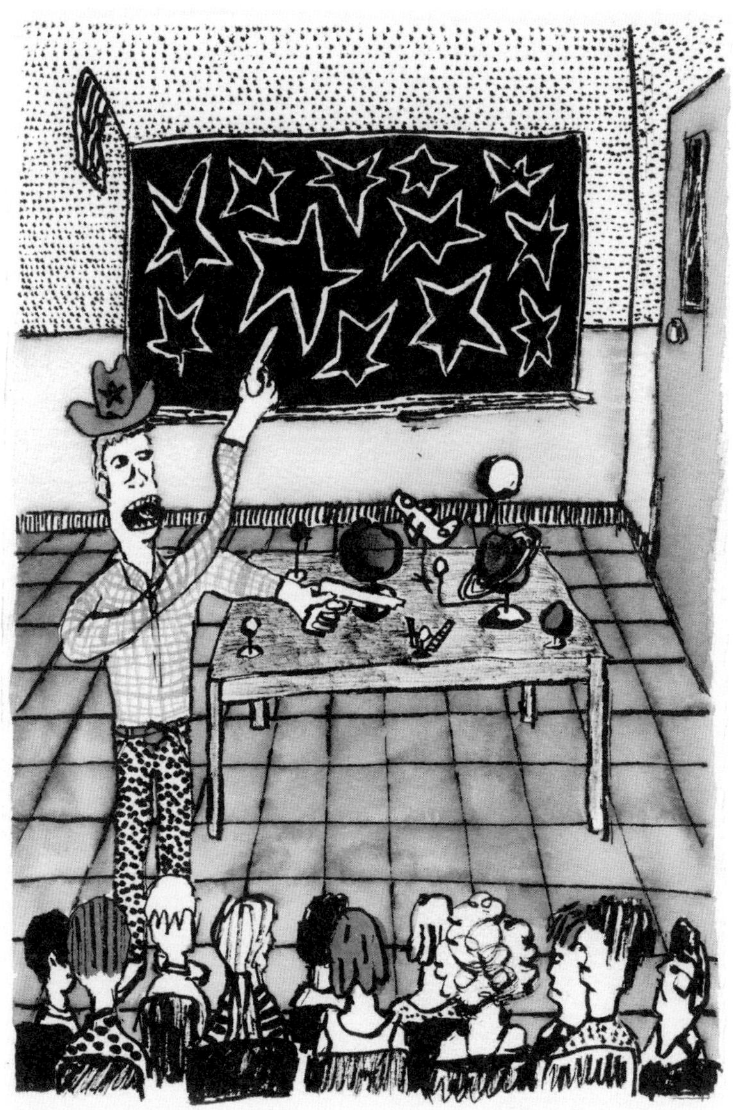

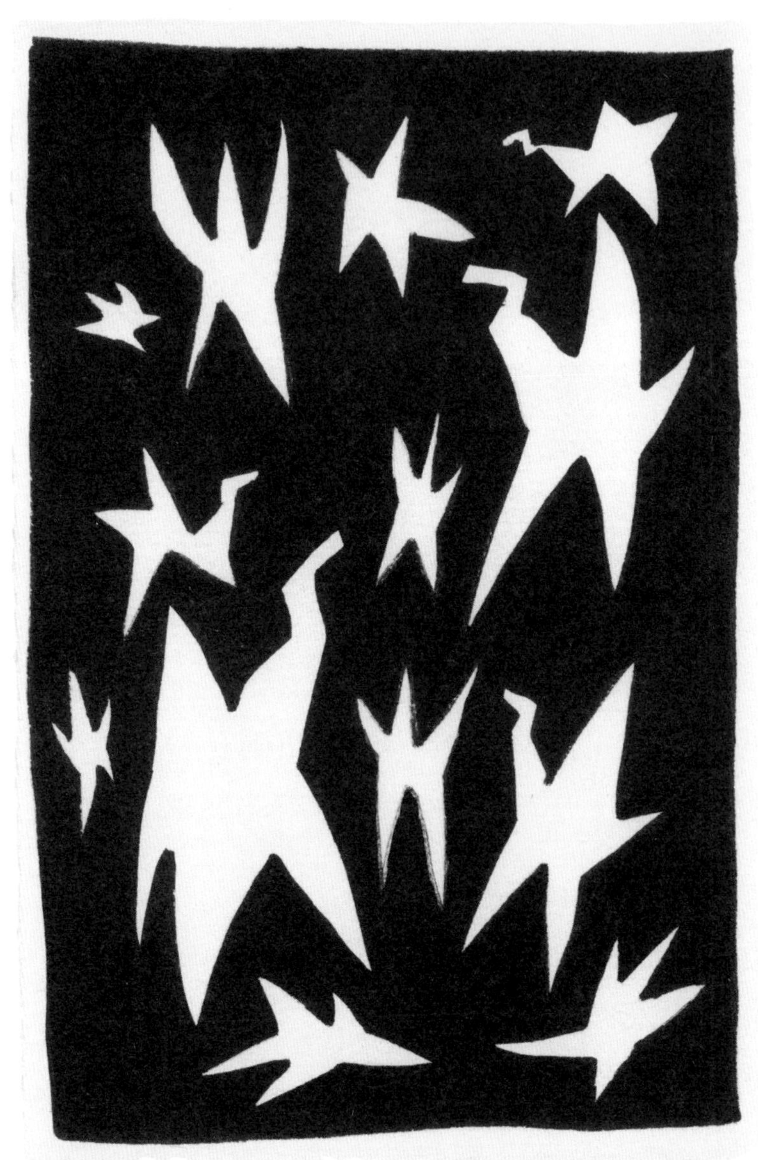

This scenario stuck itself behind my eyes and wouldn't go away until I brought it to life on a piece of paper. I started to make drawings combining the gun and the star. I drew images of people shooting the stars out at night, and stars shooting at people as target practice. Stars were shooting at other stars, black stars shooting white ones, and whites shooting blacks. The drawings became a way for me to process this complex and violent issue through a non-rational logic. I wanted to meditate on the interaction between the two symbols of guns and stars, recognising the power of both.

When drawing, I find myself jumping logic, connecting things together that produce unexpected outcomes that could not be reached with linguistic thought. There is space to play with visual elements in a constant feedback loop. Each mark on the page introduces a new idea for reexamination; drawing is thinking in physical form. It is thinking through a thing – in other words, *thinging*. While thinging, we encounter gaps in reason because when we think of a thing, it's never the same as trying to make it in reality. And when things exist in reality they produce unexpected thoughts.

But how could I make sense of these two things together, stars and guns? Guns symbolise violence and death. The star is a transcendental space, an experience to share out of a peaceful joy with others. What could it mean to be together with something that seemed to go against connection?

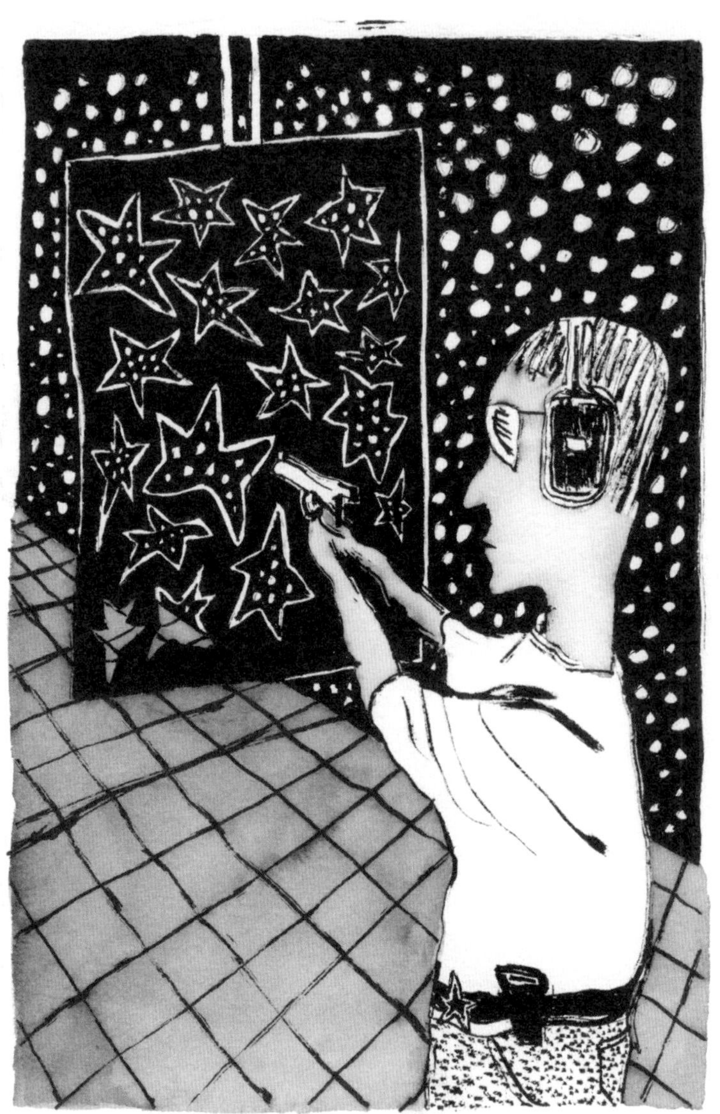

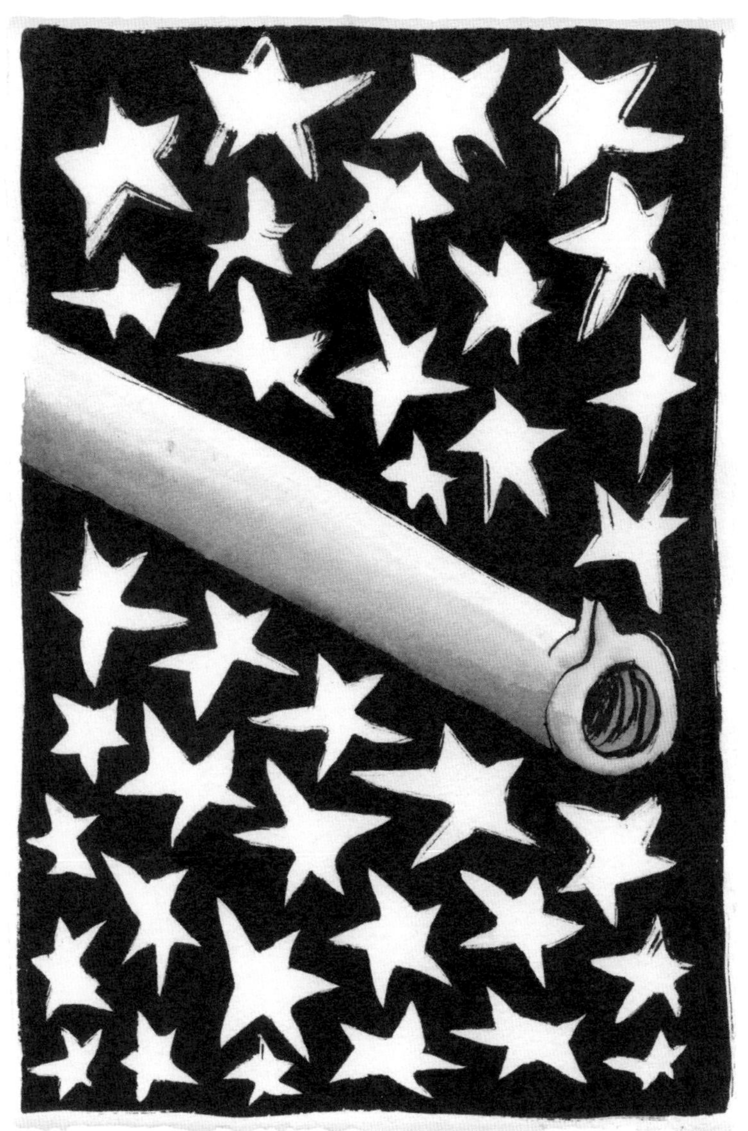

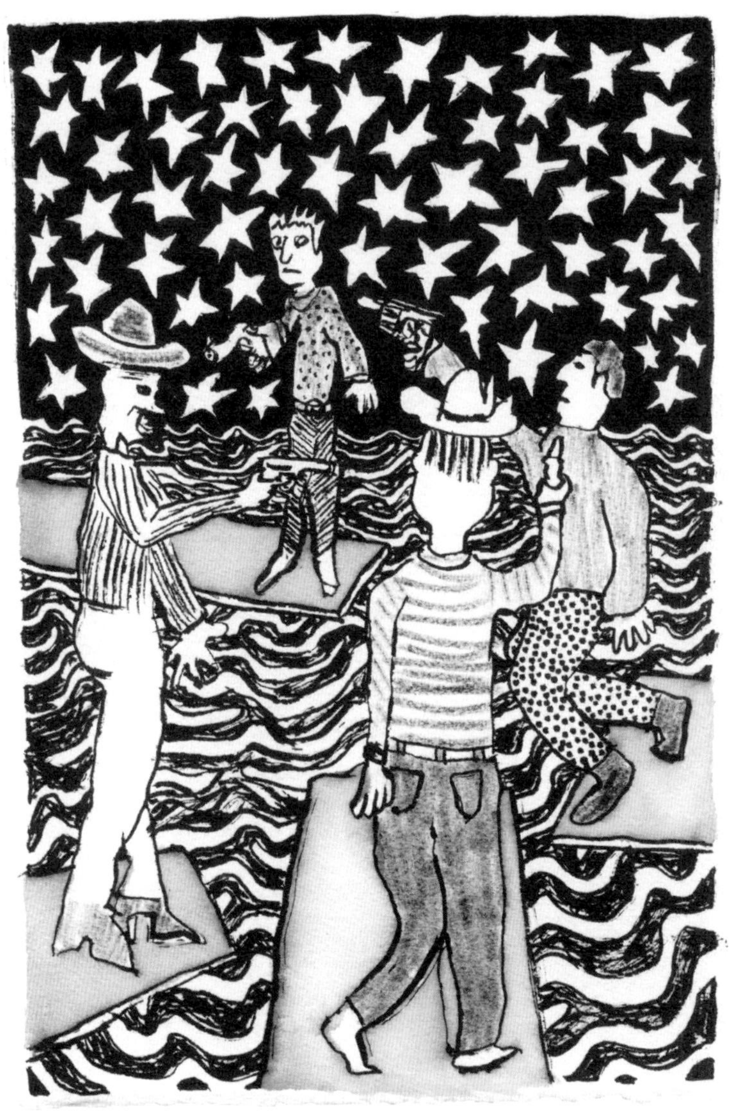

Then there is the standoff, this cinematic moment when people are pointing guns at each other, frozen and waiting to shoot. They could stand there for hours, paralysed in a tense state of contemplation. As long as no one pulls the trigger, they are suspended in a kind of togethercss, even if it is a sort of Cold War perverse togetherness. And just imagine if there are five gunslingers standing together in the standoff, their arms raised with guns in each hand. They might form the shape of a large five-pointed star, guns touching end to end. They would look like a group of nervous synchronised swimmers. They might even stand there for the rest of their lives.

If I talk to people in Europe, they don't understand why so many people in the United States are buying guns. I don't think I have a good answer. Maybe people are trying to protect themselves from the unknown. Or maybe the reason is imaginary, a fantastic cosmic reason. Perhaps there are people who are buying guns to shoot stars instead. Like a fairy with a magic wand, this gun contains magic star bullets of collective desire. It makes holes in things to allow for more airflow, because we all know that love is in the air.

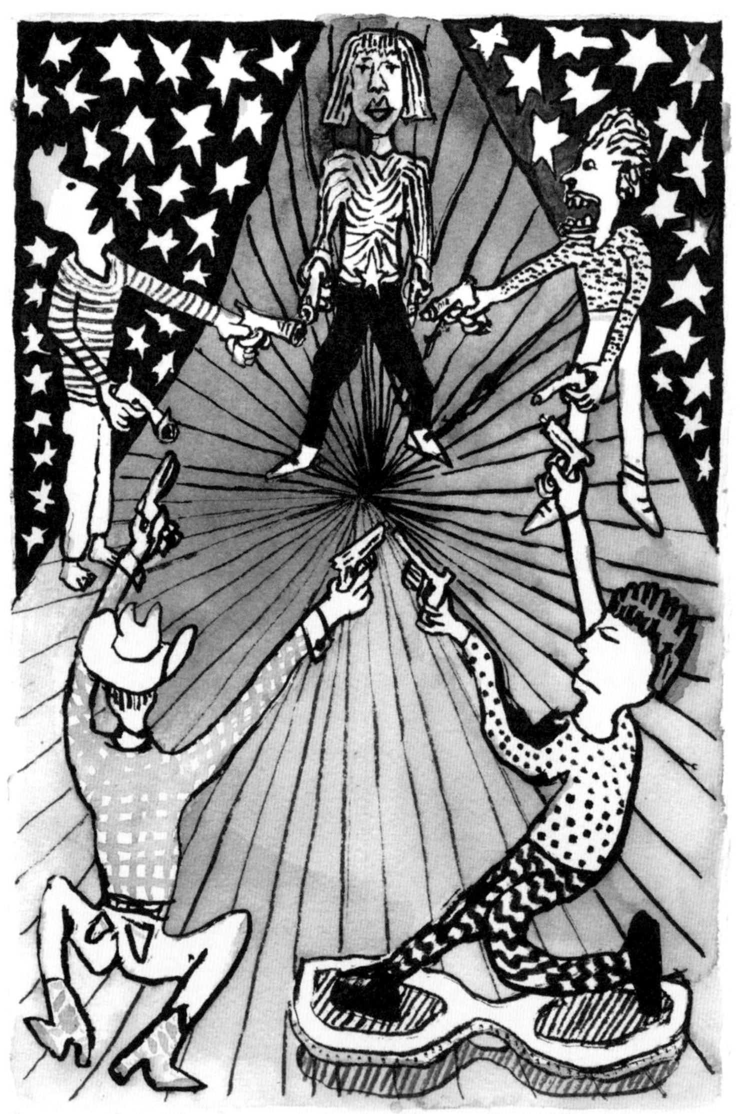

The logic that I find while drawing guns and stars is a dream logic, the logic that happens when you are asleep. The artist Agnes Martin once said in an interview that smart people say, 'I'll sleep on it' when they have to make an important decision. Because when you sleep, you give your rational mind a break and your dream logic has time to process your thoughts. Some gun owners literally sleep on it too, because they keep their guns hidden under their pillows. Like worry dolls, baby teeth, laurel leaves, and other superstitions, if you place it under your pillow, it might become charged with a special magic.

Combined with the star, the gun enters a transcendental space of the unknown, beyond clear comprehension and normal perception. The shooting star is an oxymoron, a joyful contradiction with potential both for violence and peaceful meditation. The shooting star is then a pause, a question, a proposition; opening up a space for doubt.

Nick Norton

Only One Silver Teapot

The sea was breaking heavily.
Struck violently at every wave,
the vessel drifted helplessly
among the breakers.

Two of the boats were stove in at
the outset, and the third, in which
three men were lowered, was injured
and cast ashore in the midst of
the breakers.

At the edge of the sea we have
begun to construct a topography
of knowledge.

The shape of information feeds
how such information is transformed
into useful knowledge.

Reception thus shapes perception.
Perceiving also shapes receiving.

It is a self-rewarding feedback:
receiving – getting a grip on –
holding – reading – these inward
modes are primary to any outward
motions of agency – creativity.

But to create is a slippery
business. If we are to be sure on
how and where to move, is it good to
make systems of knowing based on
gliding and sliding? A library of
slippage. The shelves are dripping.
The steps are slimy.

A map of the maybe. There is
no compass and the wind rips
apart the legend, contour lines
unravel to reveal a bowl of
overcooked spaghetti.

The sign of good order is that it
will appear natural, as if no hand
has ever touched it. Do we notice
the order things are put in? Good
order runs so smoothly that it seems
unjust to even suggest it is an
artificial construct. The question
now is to what extent we trust
the creators of these systems
which shape the feedback between
perception and reception.

Any new element in the system
forces a set of choices: does one
do violence to the system or does
one do violence to the new element?
Does one ignore the newness
precisely in order to honour the
system or does one dishonour the
system by adapting it to the new
element? Does one cut off the anchor
in order to float, or does one rely
on the weighty frame even if this
hard won stability allows dangerous
waters to overwhelm the deck?

They hastened on, witnessing the
misfortune.

At three o'clock a lifeboat was
got afloat. It was the women who
had to wade well into the water
so as to get it afloat. The men
in the boat heaved on the oars,
pushing through the swell in hope
of effecting a rescue. It was
to be a fruitless endeavour. The
lifeboat had to return to shore,
and a message was sent to the
nearest lifeboat station in order
to fetch a rocket apparatus.

The tide is rising.

I am sitting. I am holding this book
open. My back is straight. I hang my
head down, hands open beneath this
book. This book has a topography.
This book; all great swirling pools
and sharp rocks, banked up behind
it there are mountainous dunes.
The dunes are shifting all the time;
the tides are coming and going.
All the time, this land is moving.

Beyond the dunes there are
fresh water lakes and the fish
are numerous.

Life here is unique and beautiful.
The tide is rising. I look up
from the book. The book has been
pulled from a shelf. The shelf
has been slotted into a piece
of architecture. The architecture
has been raised upon the generosity
of patrons, the subscriptions of
the public, the aspirations and
movements of a misted-over history.
After the storm there will be a fog.

The accident of architecture.
The purposeful shelf. A sequence
of the possible.

To be encouraged to scratch at a
text is to be encouraged to dig.
The library is a scratching place.
The old ones lift their cold feet
in sodden socks onto the hot pipes.
The alcove begins to smell of
warmed flesh.

We scratch because there is
something happening below the
surface. A rash develops. It is
appearance itself which is itchy.

The skin must be sensed. The
eruptions will be observed or not
observed: touched, felt, caressed…
for caring is not the same as making
numb. The numb flesh ceases to be
rubbed. The cold ones curl up and
stiffen… to die into

unknowing
to return knowing
unknowing.

The non-fabulous fabulist has made
a power grab. Vanity is enforced,

the mirror that will not lie is
smashed. Yet the broken reflections
still speak. They say: 'The fairest
of them all hides in the forest.'

Perhaps the forest itself reflects
our gaze? We see in our self, seen
through the trees, the forest.

At the edge of the forest we
begin to construct a topography
of knowledge.

The shape of information feeds how
that information is transformed into
useful knowledge, and so reception
shapes perception. And perceiving
shapes receiving. And receiving
– getting a grip on – holding
– reading – these inward modes
are primary to any outward motions
of agency – creativity. Question
now how it is that we trust the
mapmakers, the signage on shelving,
the makers of good progression, and
the rewards given to children who
salvage life from sinking ships.

In the book I find an account of how
the lifeboat was launched once more,
late in the night, they pushed the
wooden boat out into furious waters.
It may have been dawn but the storm
obliterated any attempt at daylight.
The women forced their men through
the surf, and the men in the boat
succeeded in getting alongside the
steamer and saving the crew.

I feel my flesh collapse into the
account I am reading. I cry out in
amazement at the tenacity and the
generosity of this small community.
The shipwrecked people are received
in a most friendly manner, they
are now sheltering in the topography
of knowledge.

The forest is cleared. All that is
left of the forest is a woodland
which runs along the valley bottom.
This wooded area is called 'the
green belt'. It ties up the town's
trousers. When the pants get too
tight a bit more of the woodland
is cleared. The belt is getting less
as the garment is enlarged.

Father shows me the pile of rubble
left over from building the rest of
the estate. This is where our house
is going to be built. The house is
built. I grow up here.

Father comes into the room, he
tiptoes in wearing slippers and
dressing gown. He runs the flat of
his palm along my back. I struggle
to wake up. I wake up and turn
around saying; Yes? But he is gone.
The room has gone. I am awake in
my home. I walk into the stream
and lie in it under the water.
Underwater I begin a conversation
with a fish; a huge grey green carp
with no tail. 'Where is your tail?'
I ask. He says: 'Now there is a
tale for you to write. The tale of
tail.' And he swims away and I swim
after him, swimming with a newt-like
doggy paddle, skimming the gravel of
the streambed. The fish leaps up the
waterfalls. I wonder how it can do
this without a tail. The fish is all
muscle. It does swim upstream and
I am to follow it. All throughout
this conversation with the fish there
has been with us an image of a
bright shiny sword blade and I have
been holding it and not holding it.
And now I realise that the fish tail
is also the handle, so when I grab
the fish tail I can lift the sword
aloft. We have reached the highest
pool. Salmon in great abundance are

transforming and breeding and dying
all around me. The carp now tells
me that the sword is mine to take.
I stand and wade out of the pool
with the sword. I am naked. The fish
carcasses are skinned and made into
trousers for me. I am attacked by a
knight who mocks me, saying that he
will teach me how to use the sword.
Is he really teaching or really
attacking? Either way — we fight and
I cut open his legs and break his
sword and cut open his armour and
he sews fish skins together for me
in humble obedience.

Grabbing the fish tail sword is carpe
diem. Carpe is of carp — to pick
or pluck. Diem is day. This day
of carpe is also deus — deity
— the daylight sky. The sky is a
mirror. Plucking the day, touching
god, picking up a shard of a broken
mirror and seeing in it an entire
landscape. Yet the day remains
ungraspable as it is flowing, it
is chronos. We also are flowing in
time and cannot step out of this
in order to apprehend an objective
manner of reception.

A touching incident deserves
special mention. Let us step back
in order to appreciate how it was
with this little pale child who,
wet through on a cold night, rushed
along the beach, wading through
several bays by the way, and at
length reached the next lifeboat
station. It was this child who
brought back the rocket equipment,
they who enabled the next stage
of the rescue attempt.

If you trust the system that guides
you over the map, as if it were
the landscape itself, then all other

routes cease. Land and map collapse
into a single possibility; one's mode
of travel has become unconscious.

If the system is intended to be a map
of the landscape then the map cannot
claim precedent.

The morning was very dark and stormy,
and all credit is due to this child.
It is right that a reward is to be
given, it is right that it should
be awarded to those who merit it.
A silver teapot is the reward.
A very handsome solid silver teapot.
A beautiful silver teapot in a
handsome wooden case.

It turns out that these are merely
differing accounts of the same thing.
There was only one silver teapot.

Reference material from the *Morpeth Herald*, 12 July 2015:
http://www.morpethherald.co.uk/news/disaster-at-sea-witnessed-by-a-village-1-7350672

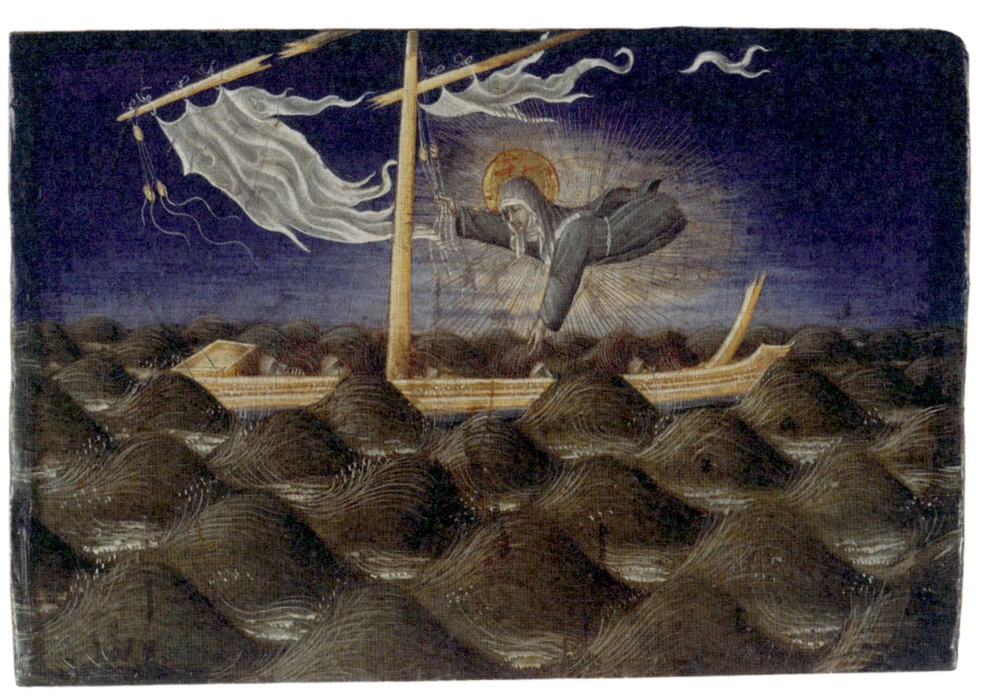

Say what you see

Portrait of Derrick May, 1995
photographed by Tai Shani

Tai Shani

See what you hear

India Arie, 'Little Things', from *Voyage to India*, 2002
https://youtu.be/gRkixkjQIAw

Jim

There's this game where every once in a while you try to say or do some nonsense. It can be harder than you think, especially if you try it in a room full of well-humoured people who are very open to all sorts of cues and just make everything part of a conversation. Ideally this journal is like that, everyone in great spirits just having a conversation.

It started with this one situation in a market in Vilnius where one woman working there was talking – very loudly, for everyone to hear – about some very hospitable man in Georgia with a house full of books. She said that he'd invited her and her friends to his house and she asked if he had read all these books, to which he replied: 'Oh I have read all your Tolstoyevskys!'

A friend told his story at a dinner and we all laughed at it, we still do, but it appears we all laughed at different things and even at different people. Did the man say he reads stuff although he doesn't, or did he say he doesn't read? Someone thought he was neither lying nor joking but said he reads *different* books, and others believed he had honestly made a mistake. Some of us got the story wrong entirely.

The main portion of this magazine is based on an open call for submissions, an invitation to write something between the Tolstoyevsky story (also see the back cover) and 'Moles & Mice' by Candice Lin (published here on p.8). The rest are contributions that came about in conversations with the artist Elena Narbutaitė, whom we called Flow Editor: short stories by David Bernstein, Monika Kalinauskaitė and Jonas Žakaitis, collages by ateate and other images, which all turned this issue into a house full of books and conversations where saying nonsense is almost entirely impossible.

Tolstoyevsky is not a Russian writer; it is a monster of sorts – a chimera, a composite of two and true to neither one nor a sum. It can make jokes (and threats) fly so fast they skip the funny parts. Here it lends its name to an issue that is about how humour is often not humour, or about how it sometimes doesn't work, and how half of our lives are filled with things that don't work. Which probably means they work, right?

— Virginija Januškevičiūtė

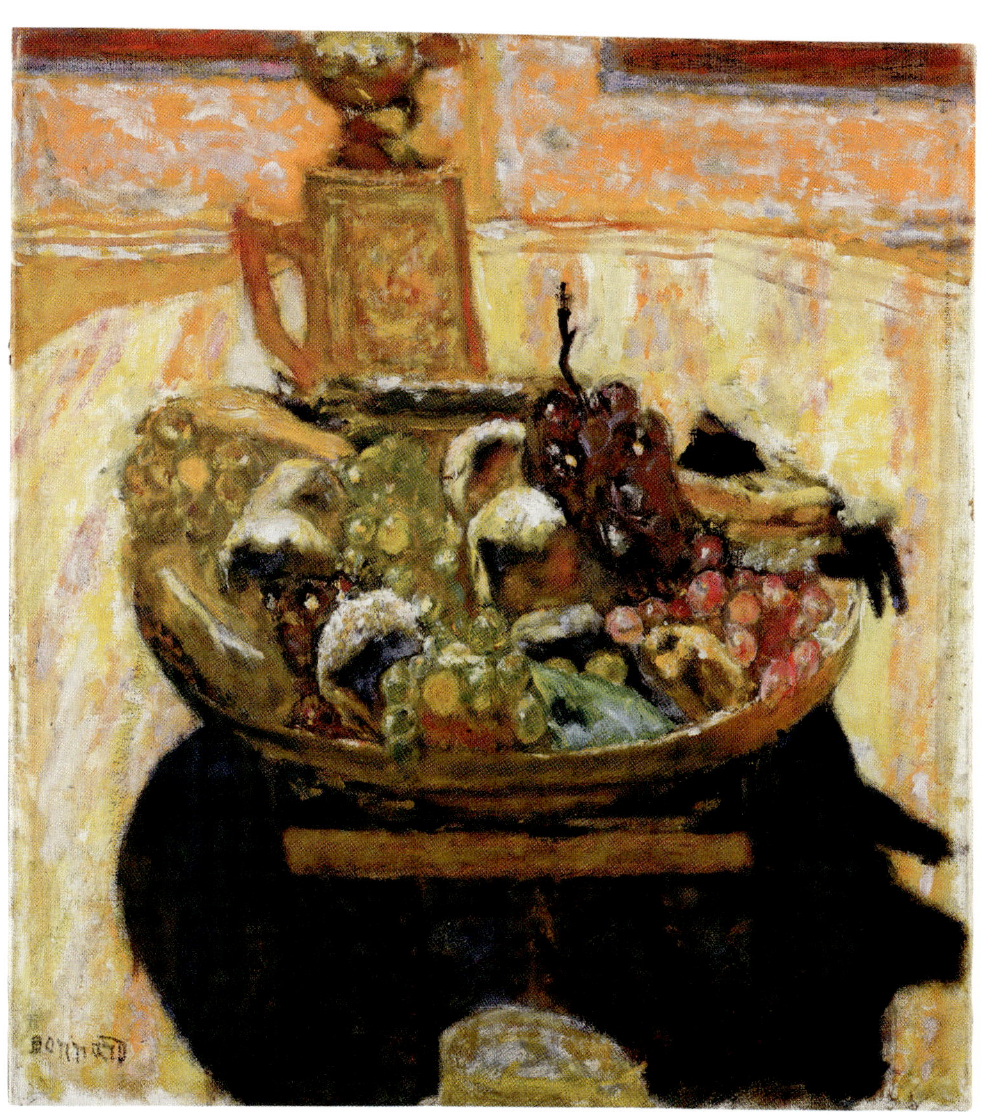

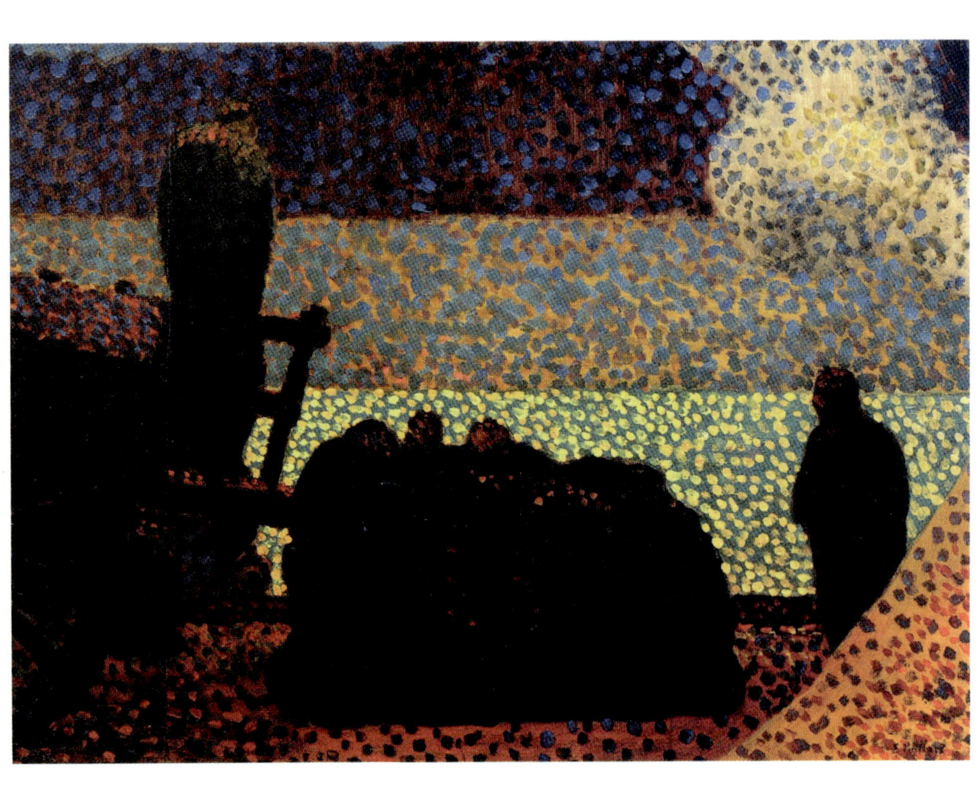

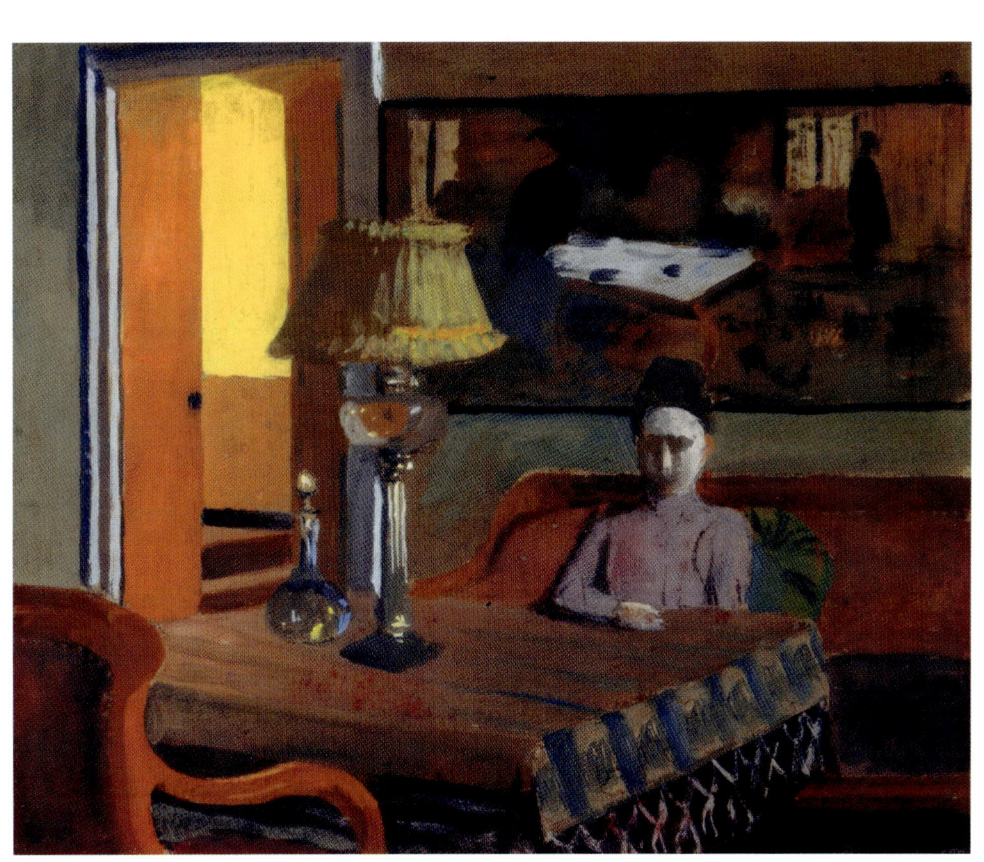

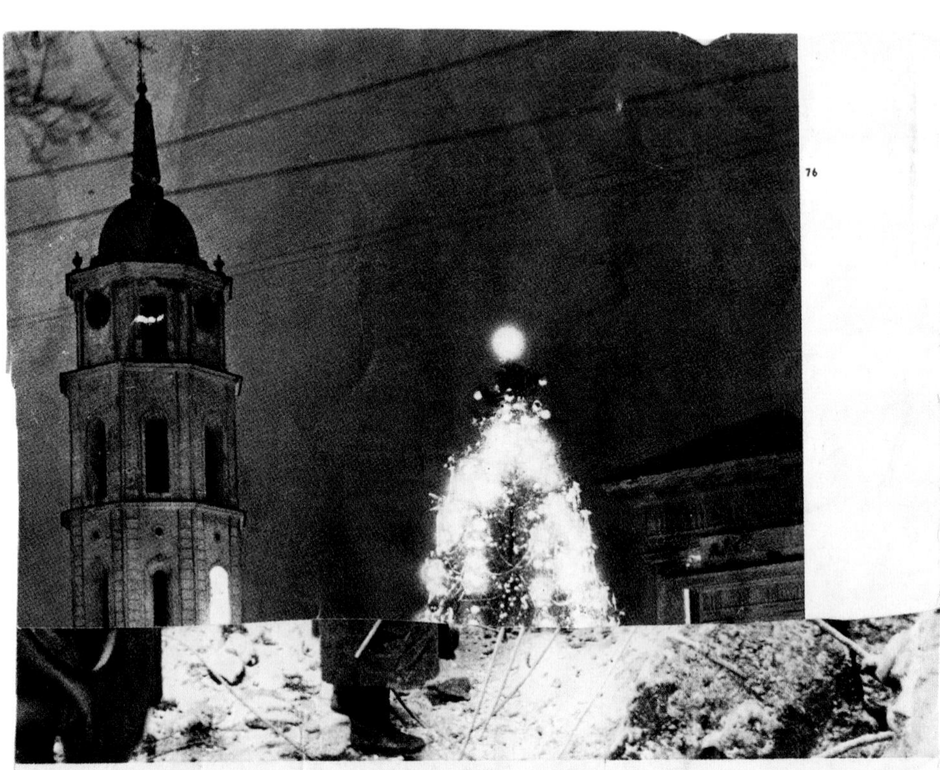

POLSCY ŻOŁNIERZE W ZDOBYTYCH BUNKRACH WAŁU POMORSKIEGO *fot. arch.*

ateate

First, we meet inside of all things. / We meet alone or with the team / To feel the nullity, / To let go of the reins. / Surrender to the force, to swirl around like dust. / Then. / It begins. / The sense. / Of losing ourselves. / Our bodies just string marionettes. / And us expanding into giant viewers. / Who always wonder. / And the result, we get, turns out to be the side effect. / A message to us, to you. / So unexpected, so intense / Or sometimes a message that is – / Ah! So common, so intimate, so known. / The sense of action, / The move without control to us is pure joy. / We let our works be separate from us, be bodies on their own.

David Bernstein

b. 1988, San Antonio, Texas, is an artist based in Amsterdam and Brussels. He combines performance, sculpture, and writing to tell stories through objects. He likes to touch things and is obsessed with spatulas and Fiat Multiplas. From 2015 to 2016 he was a resident at the Jan van Eyck Academy in Maastricht. Before that, he studied at the Sandberg Institute in Amsterdam.

Maria Fusco

is a Belfast born writer based in Glasgow, and Research Fellow at the Amsterdam Centre for Cultural Analysis, University of Amsterdam in 2018. She is Editorial Director of *The Happy Hypocrite*, and Reader at the University of Edinburgh. James Elkins has said of her new book of critical writings *Give up Art* (New Documents, 2018): 'after a book like this, most nonfiction seems curiously unaware of what writing can be', and Chris Kraus has called her recent book *Legend of the Necessary Dreamer* (Vanguard Editions, 2017) 'a new classic of female philosophical fiction'.

Virginija Januškevičiūtė

is a contemporary art curator, writer and producer based in Vilnius who engages in a wide range of solo and group exhibitions, artwork commissions, publications and events. She works at the Contemporary Art Centre in Vilnius (www.cac.lt) and is founding co-editor of The Baltic Notebooks of Anthony Blunt (www.blunt.cc). She curated the XII Baltic Triennial in 2015.

Monika Kalinauskaitė

is a writer and curator based in Vilnius, Lithuania. She regularly publishes fiction, essays and reviews in Lithuanian and international cultural press, and her textual works have been featured in group shows and assorted artistic projects. She recently co-authored *The Great Outdoors* (TLTRPreß, Berlin), a graphic novel interrogating the Lovecraftian nuances of human intimacy, and is currently curating the Reading Room collection and programming at the Contemporary Art Centre in Vilnius.

Zoe Kingsley

is a writer and collaborator recently returned to Melbourne. Her poetry and art writing have been published in *Powder Keg*, *Textual Practice* and *Cosmonauts Avenue*. She is co-deputy editor of literary and arts journal *The Suburban Review*.

Erika Lastovskyte

is a translator, publicist, and rights professional, currently living in Oxford, UK. She received her MA in English Studies from Vilnius University, and has worked on the Summer Literary Seminars and Baltic Women Writers' Tour. Erika has been awarded the individual stipend from the Lithuanian Council for Culture for promotion of Lithuanian literature in the English speaking countries, and the prestigious Emerging Translator Mentorships Programme organised by Writers' Centre Norwich.

Michael Lawton
is an artist and writer. Born in Sheffield in
1980 he currently lives and works in Barcelona.
Lawton is in the final year of a PhD in Fine Art
at the University of Kent, previously having
studied at Chelsea College of Art & Design,
the University of Huddersfield and Leeds
Metropolitan University. The hypothesis of
his research is that the best writing to accompany
an artwork is a work of fiction; narratives that
exist in the world the viewer enters when they
encounter the artwork, texts written for paintings
rather than about them. The story included
here was written for the Romanesque Murals
in the Museu Nacional d'Art de Catalunya.

Candice Lin
engages notions of gender, race and sexuality
in her work, drawing from post/de-colonialism,
citizen science, anthropology, feminist and
queer theory. Lin has exhibited widely including
recent shows at Moderna Museet (Stockholm),
the New Museum (NY), HANGAR (Lisbon),
Sculpture Center (NY), Galeria Fortes Vilaça
(São Paulo), with recent residencies and awards
at Centre les Récollets (2017), Headlands Center
for the Arts (2016) and the Louis Comfort
Tiffany Foundation Award (2017). Her recent
solo exhibitions were at Betonsalon in 2017,
Gasworks (London) and Commonwealth &
Council (LA) in 2016.

Elena Narbutaitė
we should call her.

Nick Norton
has published poetry and prose. His book
AKA: A Genealogy of the Saddle, commissioned
by Book Works, is described by the filmmaker
Patrick Keiller as 'a joy to read, Nick Norton's
wonderful book brings a headlong, associative
sensibility to the literature of landscape. I wish
there were more books like it.' Norton helped
collaboratively set up the artist group Inventory,

publishing and exhibiting with them until 2003.
He conceived Library Interventions in 2013 and
has curated various Interventions in the context
of an academic art library. He continues to write,
even though it is way past his bedtime.

Kim Schoen
lives and works in Los Angeles and Berlin.
Her work in photography, video installation, and
text takes on the rhetorics of display in consumer
culture. Select international exhibitions include
LAXART, South London Gallery, Whitechapel
Gallery, MOT International, and MMoCA.
Her work has been written about in the *LA Times*,
Artforum, *Mousse*, and *Art in America*, and she has
published her own writing on repetition and
photography in *X-TRA Contemporary Art Quarterly*.
Kim is also the co-founder and co-editor of
MATERIAL, a journal of writing by contemp-
orary artists. She is represented by Moskowitz
Bayse in Los Angeles.

Isabel Waidner
is a writer and cultural theorist. She is the
author of three books of innovative fiction, most
recently *Gaudy Bauble* (Dostoyevsky Wannabe,
2017). Her articles and short fictions have
appeared in journals including *3:AM*, *Berfrois*,
Configurations, and *Minor Literature[s]*. A founding
member of the indie band Klang, Waidner
released records on UK labels Rough Trade
(2003) and Blast First (2004). She is a lecturer
in English and Creative Writing at Roehampton
University and the organiser of an event series
on queer writing at the Centre for Feminist
Research at Goldsmiths, University of London.

Jonas Žakaitis
is a writer based in Vilnius, Lithuania. He recently
published *90s*, his first collection of short stories
(www.90s.lt). His writings have also been published
in various artist publications and contemporary art
magazines. He has participated in numerous contemporary art projects as a gallerist and a curator.

ERICA SCOURTI

The Happy Hypocrite is seeking submissions for future issues.
Next Guest Editor: Erica Scourti
For more information please visit: bookworks.org.uk/news,
or join our mailing list at: bookworks.org.uk/contact

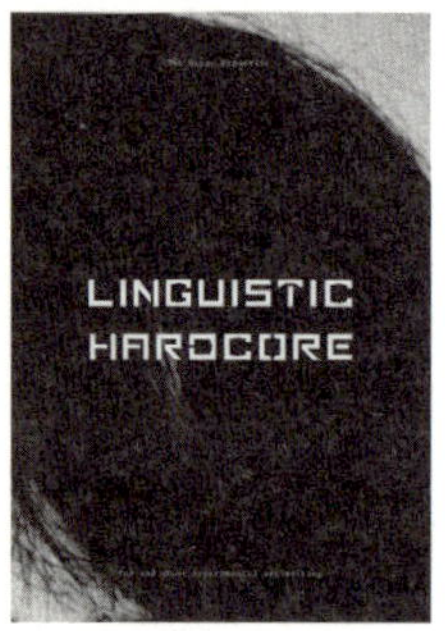

Issue 1
'Linguistic Hardcore'
Spring / Summer 2008

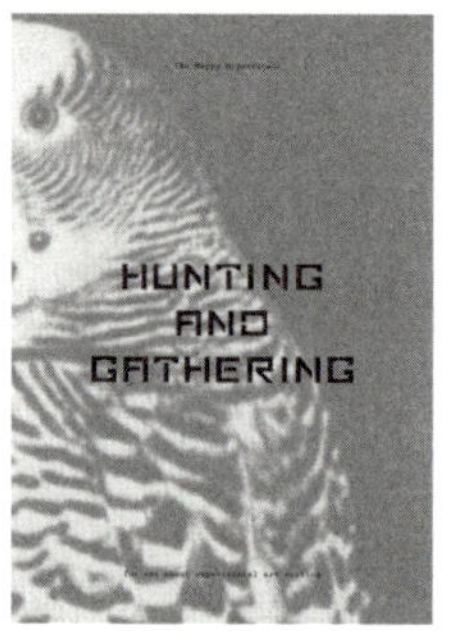

Issue 2
'Hunting and Gathering'
Autumn / Winter 2008

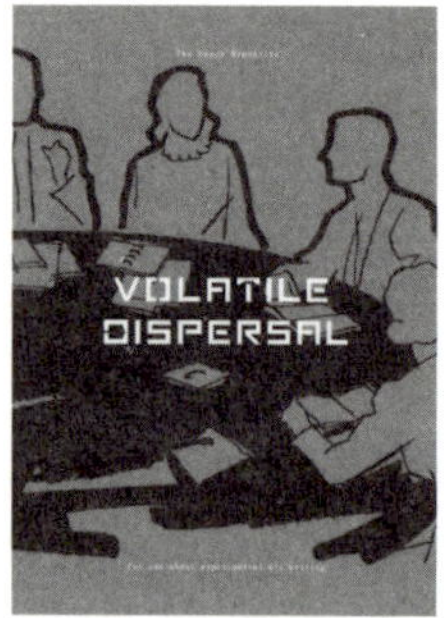

Issue 3
'Volatile Dispersal'
Spring / Summer 2009

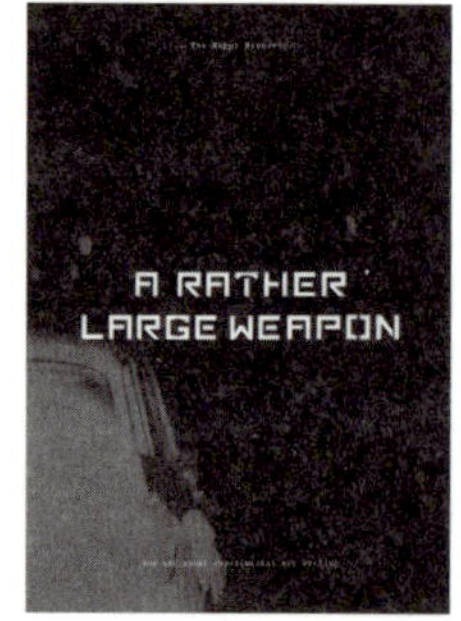

Issue 4
'A Rather Large Weapon'
Autumn / Winter 2009

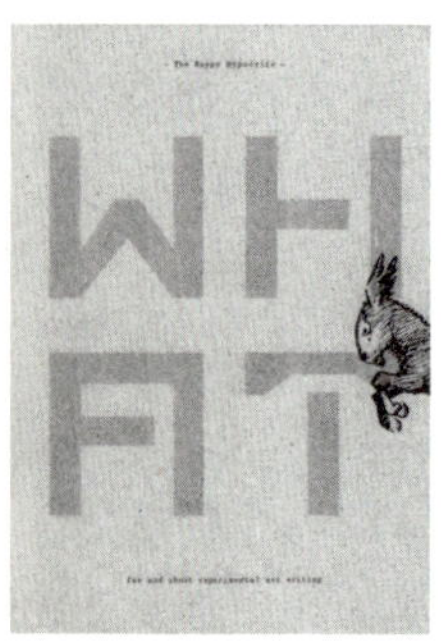

Issue 5
'What am I?'
Spring / Summer 2010

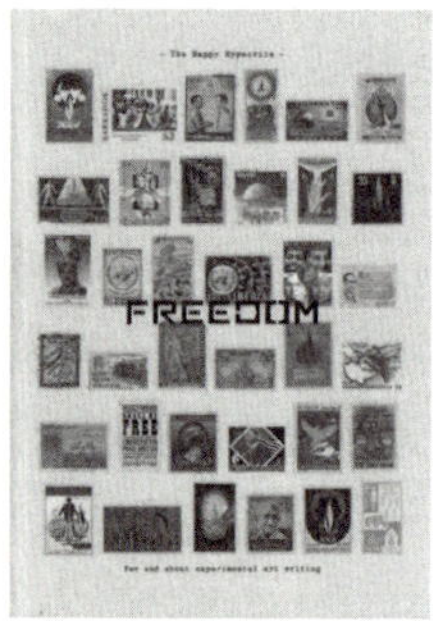

Issue 6
'Freedom'
Guest edited by Lynne Tillman
Autumn 2013

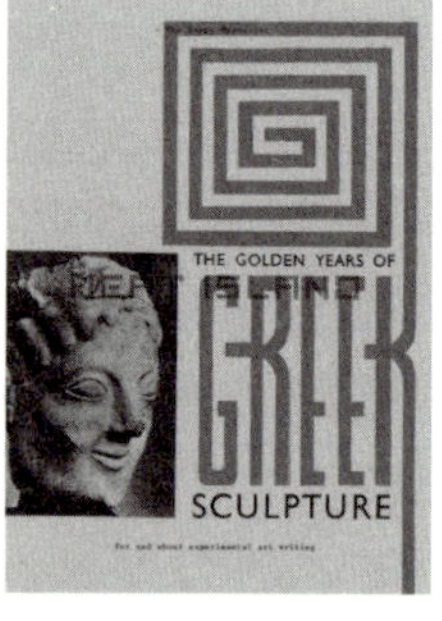

Issue 7
'Heat Island'
Guest edited by
Mason Leaver-Yap
Autumn 2014

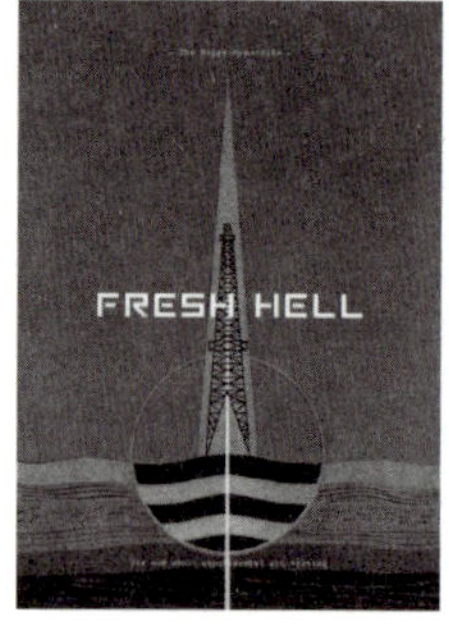

Issue 8
'Fresh Hell'
Guest edited by Sophia Al-Maria
Autumn 2015

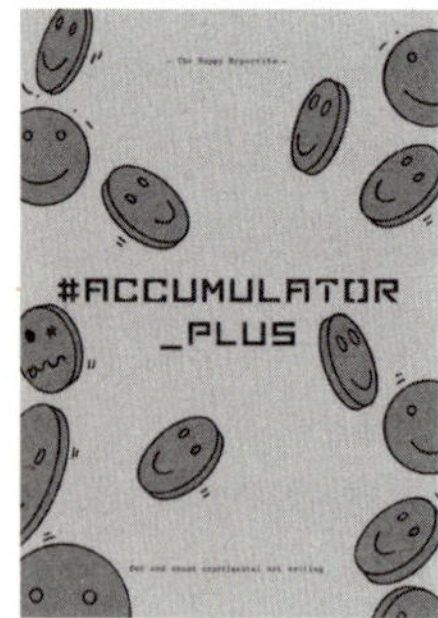

Issue 9
'#ACCUMULATOR_PLUS'
Guest edited by Hannah Sawtell
Autumn 2016

Available to order from bookworks.org.uk